Accelerating N Literacy

This book supports educators in teaching academic writing skills to Newcomer English Learners (ELs) who are just beginning their English language learning journey.

Newcomer ELs typically have minimal familiarity with the English alphabet, which can be an obstacle for them when learning writing, phonics, and spelling in English. Drawing on research and classroom-tested methods, this book provides teachers practical strategies to help Newcomers start writing earlier, mastering letter-sound correspondence, and gaining confidence to write their thoughts in English. Readers will learn how to seamlessly integrate EL-targeted strategies and personalized literacy instruction into writing workshops to accelerate Newcomer's acquisition of English phonics, spelling, and writing skills. These adaptable strategies also benefit world language teachers seeking effective ways to teach writing and literacy to beginners on any language learning journey.

Built on the author's instructional coaching expertise and observations of field testing by practicing teachers, this is an excellent resource for English as a Second Language (ESL) educators and instructional coaches to promote faster and better literacy acquisition for their Newcomers and other beginner language learners.

Eugenia Krimmel is an English Language Development Instructional Coach and Consultant. She has over 30 years of experience as an ESOL educator and has taught ESL and EFL in the Middle East, Europe, Canada, and the United States.

Accelerating Newcomer Literacy

An Integrated Writing Process Playbook for English Learners

Eugenia Krimmel

Routledge
Taylor & Francis Group

NEW YORK AND LONDON

Designed cover image: © Getty Images

First published 2026
by Routledge
605 Third Avenue, New York, NY 10158

and by Routledge
4 Park Square, Milton Park, Abingdon, Oxon, OX14 4RN

Routledge is an imprint of the Taylor & Francis Group, an informa business

© 2026 Taylor & Francis

The right of Eugenia Krimmel to be identified as author of this work has
been asserted in accordance with sections 77 and 78 of the Copyright,
Designs and Patents Act 1988.

ISBN: 978-1-041-00584-1 (hbk)
ISBN: 978-1-041-00583-4 (pbk)
ISBN: 978-1-003-61059-5 (ebk)

DOI: 10.4324/9781003610595

Typeset in Optima
by Apex CoVantage, LLC

Access the Support Material: www.routledge.com/9781041005834

Accelerating Newcomer Literacy

An Integrated Writing Process Playbook for English Learners

Eugenia Krimmel

R Routledge
Taylor & Francis Group

NEW YORK AND LONDON

Designed cover image: © Getty Images

First published 2026
by Routledge
605 Third Avenue, New York, NY 10158

and by Routledge
4 Park Square, Milton Park, Abingdon, Oxon, OX14 4RN

Routledge is an imprint of the Taylor & Francis Group, an informa business

© 2026 Taylor & Francis

The right of Eugenia Krimmel to be identified as author of this work has
been asserted in accordance with sections 77 and 78 of the Copyright,
Designs and Patents Act 1988.

ISBN: 978-1-041-00584-1 (hbk)
ISBN: 978-1-041-00583-4 (pbk)
ISBN: 978-1-003-61059-5 (ebk)

DOI: 10.4324/9781003610595

Typeset in Optima
by Apex CoVantage, LLC

Access the Support Material: www.routledge.com/9781041005834

To those Newcomer English and Multilingual Learners who courageously navigate the world in more than one language, striving to learn, grow, and thrive across cultures. And to the teachers who dedicate themselves to guiding others through the beauty and complexity of bilingual and multilingual life, especially in those first few steps of that journey.

To my parents, whose decision to send me across the world as a teenager set me on a path of discovery – of language, culture, and purpose. That journey shaped not only my life but also this work, a testament to the power of adaptation and resilience.

To my husband and children, whose unwavering support consistently fuels my passion for language and learning. May their world – and the world of future generations – be one of understanding, global community, and peace.

Contents

Appendices   169

Meet the Author

Meet Dr. Eugenia Krimmel, an accomplished ESOL educator, presenter, instructional coach, and policymaker whose passion for language learning was sparked during her own teenage student exchange experience in Turkey. Navigating the challenges and triumphs of learning a new language firsthand, Eugenia is dedicated to empowering beginner language learners through the process of transforming English letters and words into meaningful writing. She has taught preschool, high school, college and adult ESOL in Turkey, Spain, Canada, Florida, and in her home state of Pennsylvania before earning her Master of Education, ESOL Specialty from the Universidad del Turabo, Puerto Rico, and later her doctorate in educational leadership from Immaculata University.

As a Fellow of the National Writing Project, Dr. Krimmel actively contributes to advancing writing instruction. She has a distinguished career as an ESOL presenter at TESOL, WIDA, and PennTESOL conferences on topics like ELD curriculum development and ESOL best practices. Eugenia worked extensively with state and federal policymakers and thought leaders as the ESL/bilingual advisor in the Pennsylvania Department of Education. That work led her to a new frontier – cyber school ESOL. She is currently the ESL instructional coach at a large cyber school where she trains over 2,400 teachers on how to effectively educate multilingual learners in a fully online learning environment.

Eugenia is a teacher contributor to Vista Higher Learning's new ESOL high school book series and has worked on ESOL benchmark testing for a district in Tennessee based on ELPA21 standards. In her book, Dr. Krimmel offers practical insights and proven methods to help teachers engage

Newcomers in language learning step by step to achieve linguistic and academic success.

Now residing in Pennsylvania with her husband, she balances her professional commitments with a vibrant family life – raising three children, two of whom have embraced international cultures through marriage, while the youngest pursues graduate studies.

Acknowledgments

Maria Lo
Jessica Zielinski
Georgia Emert
Lori Funk
Elizabeth Goheen
Heather Koterwas
Jamie McGee
Anja Oberg
Emily Coleman, Ed.D.
Amanda Guzman, Director of Migrant Education Summer Camp Program
Migrant Education Program Summer Camp Staff, Educators, and Students,
    Millersville University
ESL Clinical Practicum Institute, Millersville University Staff and Graduate
    Students

Introduction

About This Book

Writing is a difficult skill for most of us to master. Now imagine having to write words and sentences in a language system you do not know. Think about it. You would communicate the wrong words and readers will not understand what you wrote. It can be frustrating. Speaking, on the other hand, develops from birth into a predictable process for most of us to communicate our thoughts through words, gestures, and sounds people around us understand. When trying to speak in a new language, we can gesture and make faces to communicate if the words are not in our minds, yet. Writing, however, is "flat" and far less of a natural development process. Literacy, reading, and writing require specific learning to achieve, especially academic-level literacy success (Pugh et al., 2001).

How then do humans learn to write in their first, second, or even fifth language? And how should you, as a teacher, provide literacy instruction for English learners who are beginning their language learning journey? Current research studies indicate that the writing process is one effective way to teach students to be good writers (Flower & Hayes, 1981; Greenwald et al., 1999; Unger & Fleischman, 2004). Students are taught how to share and communicate their ideas through steps in a process from planning, writing, and revising before publishing.

"Writing is thinking. To write well is to think clearly. That's why it's so hard", quipped David McCullough in an interview with NEH chairman Bruce Cole, *Humanities*, July/Aug. 2002, Vol. 23/No. 4. For you, teachers

DOI: 10.4324/9781003610595-1

of native and non-native English speakers, it is critical to remember that *assigning writing is not teaching writing.*

What is involved in the teaching and learning of writing? I found the research of Berninger and Winn (2006) to be clear and concise in answering that question. Table I.1 gives you a visual of their perspective in their book entitled *The Not So Simple View of Writing* (2006). Keep this graphic representation of writing in mind while reading this book and while planning your lessons.

Based on Berninger and Winn's (2006) *The Not So Simple View of Writing*, we often refer to writing as simply writing down ideas, but this visual shows us all how complex the "simple act of writing truly is" (Berninger & Winn, 2006). Even native English speakers find writing difficult; therefore, teachers must learn the art of teaching writing for all students. As you think back to your pre-service courses, how many truly taught you how to teach writing effectively for any student? And did you learn how to teach writing to culturally and linguistically diverse students?

You and I as teachers must integrate language and literacy development together. Do not wait for oral language to be in place before starting English literacy skill instruction for English learners (ELs), especially those newly arrived in the U.S. schools who are also new to the English language. These students are called Newcomers. For these culturally and

Table I.1 The Not-So-Simple View of Writing

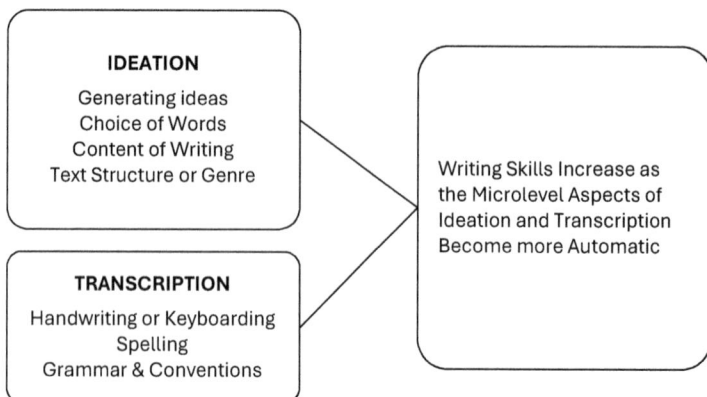

IDEATION

Generating ideas
Choice of Words
Content of Writing
Text Structure or Genre

Writing Skills Increase as the Microlevel Aspects of Ideation and Transcription Become more Automatic

TRANSCRIPTION

Handwriting or Keyboarding
Spelling
Grammar & Conventions

linguistically diverse ELs, all four language skills contribute to second language acquisition (SLA) from day one of school.

Why I Wrote This Book

As a former second language Newcomer myself, followed by 30 years of experience in English as a Second or New Language (ESL/ENL) teaching, policymaking, consulting, and instructional coaching, I have found countless teachers doing Newcomer ELs a disservice by not encouraging English writing from day one. Based on my observations, some teachers unintentionally deny Newcomers educational equity by limiting their writing practice to copying words or drawing. In my view, this deficit-based approach hinders their literacy development and delays their acquisition of written English.

For years I pondered this dilemma and how I can help fellow teachers like you learn how to teach writing effectively. I began by reflecting on my own writing instruction practice. I realized that I have been "pushing" my Newcomers to write English as much as they can from the first days in my classes. Why did I do that? Because when I was a 17-year-old exchange student to Turkey and knew no Turkish, I was encouraged to write lists, label pictures, and even write postcards very early on in this new language journey. To this day, 40 years later, I can still write in Turkish to communicate my thoughts. I was not held back or told to wait until I spoke the language, so why would I hold my Newcomer English students back from writing?

In my own experience, I had to learn Turkish in my host family's village where no one spoke any English, and I knew not one word of Turkish. Luckily, back in 1979, I was given a bilingual dictionary that helped me learn the words I wanted to say or write. The very act of searching for those words made each memorable in my brain. I learned those words faster and better than how I learned Spanish in my high school. I can even tell you how and when I learned specific words because the situations were memorable or the need for a certain word was immediate. My own second language learner Newcomer experience began my life-long career in second or new language teaching that I am sharing with you in this book.

My language teaching career truly began after graduating from college when I returned to Turkey. I lived and worked in Istanbul teaching English as a new language to children and adults for a few years. I then moved to Madrid, Spain, where I realized the way I learned Spanish for six years in school was not the best. I learned Spanish in English if you know what I mean – everything was translated, so we all knew what we were saying. I think Americans learn that way to be more comfortable, but believe me, new language learning requires uncomfortable times. According to Sousa (2010), we learn within the process of going from confusion and disequilibrium to understanding and comfort. New language learning routinely involves confusion to understanding to move words and concepts into long-term memory. More on that later in this book.

Spanish came back to me slowly, very slowly when I first arrived in Madrid. As I mentioned, I had learned Spanish in English – talking *about* the language more than talking *in* the language. Writing in Spanish was merely to fill in the blanks, but rarely did I ever write a sentence in Spanish despite having six years of instruction. The difference in my two language learning journeys taught me about the critical role writing plays in language acquisition. I was determined to become an effective ESL teacher and train others to be the same.

When I became an English as a Second Language (ESL) Program Specialist Certification Program adjunct professor over 20 years ago, I noticed my pre-service teachers received little to no training on how to teach foundational writing literacy skills such as phonics, spelling, and writing skills to any students, let alone culturally and linguistically diverse learners of any stage. I simply did not understand why that was the case. Luckily my own Master's in Education program included a six-credit course in teaching writing to ELs. That National Writing Project course truly consolidated my writing-teacher confidence and skills.

As a Fellow of the National Writing Project and ESL teacher of both high school and adult students, I searched for a systematic approach to replicate my own experience as a successful second language learner in Turkish. My career has afforded me plenty of opportunities to teach Newcomers foundational literacy skills such as phonics, spelling, and basic writing skills. Routinely I had my Newcomers writing sooner and more effectively than I had seen in most EL or content classrooms when I observed as a professor or consultant.

Having Newcomers write even letters or words to label things and then writing short sentences seemed natural to me, but my colleagues often told me their students could not write in English but only copy. I asked if they challenged their students to try both copying with comprehension and writing some words from their own thoughts. The teachers vehemently stated, "they can't write anything in English". Well, "they can't" is not in my vocabulary! I say to myself, "How can I get my Newcomers to do this writing task with my support?" That is my mantra, and I intend to shift your mindset from "they can't" to "what can I do to get them to complete a task", too!

EL-Integrated Writing Process for Educational Equity

For a moment, we will transition from my why to your why. Equity for ELs. It is a small word, equity, but truly it is multifaceted. We can only control what we can control – so we shall look to our own instructional practices and attitudes. Knowing what is deficit-based is half the battle. To turn that into assets-based thinking, always say to yourself, "This Newcomer comes with funds of knowledge like treasures I need to discover".

I read about a teacher who placed a white box high on a shelf that had the word "New" on it. He asked his class if anyone saw something new in the class. Finally, one student pointed out the white box. If they wanted to know what was inside, they had to complete the daily academic challenges he gave them as a class. The class was so interested in the unknown treasure in that box that they pulled together their funds of knowledge and eventually earned the right to reach the box. They opened it to find party supplies for a class celebration. The teacher's lesson was about explorers and discoveries in history; however, to me as a language teacher, it reminds me of the daily challenges to reach what is inside the minds of every Newcomer and EL behind the language barrier that is like something out of reach. Equity in instruction, including writing, is the path to discover the treasures within every student.

Writing, when seen as a set of shared symbols representing one's ideas in visual form, is both complex and essential in this age of information and technology. Most educators agree that writing is the most difficult skill to learn and is often called the last acquired skill for all students, especially those new to the language. Why then do teachers of beginner-level Newcomers wait an entire school year before having them write any of their own thoughts? What obstacles prevent teachers of Newcomers from initiating effective writing instruction to support their English literacy development journey?

Some teachers reason that writing represents oral language; therefore, until Newcomers develop a broader vocabulary, they cannot produce English writing on their own. Other teachers claim that the materials to teach basic writing skills like the alphabet and sight words are too childish for Newcomers in grades 3–12. Still other teachers say they do not know how to teach writing to those who have so little English and/or use a different written script. These barriers are based on ability, not equity. It can be argued that by *not* teaching Newcomers the complexities of English writing even at the word level perpetuates a delay in their English language proficiency. This book proposes a solution to this inequity issue by introducing an integrated approach to teaching beginner Newcomers the literacy subskills of phonics, spelling, and basic writing from day one within your regular writing process routine.

To start, you must remember that most ELs are fluent (orally) in their first language. Cognitively they can perform academic tasks, and, as William Randolph Hearst once quipped to a reporter, "if they can think, they can write".

In this book I introduce to you the EL Writing Process, which is a methodology founded on the premise that most Newcomers are *able* to write to the level of their peers; therefore, teachers must facilitate English writing routinely from the first day of class. My goal in writing this book is to challenge you as a writing and literacy teacher to accelerate your Newcomer's reading and writing skills beyond simply having them copy words they only mindlessly repeat. To that end, this book will fill your teaching toolkit of strategies and will build your confidence in teaching Newcomers phonics, spelling, and basic English writing, all within the writing process instruction you already do in your class! Better still, the EL Writing Process protocol is not a program with prescribed materials. Use what you have in your curriculum materials. You will learn the specific action steps you will need to accelerate your Newcomers' literacy skills in English.

The EL Writing Process Integration at a Glance

Because most ELs, according to research, develop literacy, specifically writing skills, more slowly than oral language skills in English, what can teachers do to improve the rate of ELs' literacy learning to keep pace with their oral language development? For answers, I looked to the common teaching method known as "the writing process": pre-writing, drafting, revising, editing, and publishing. By integrating EL techniques into a process you know, you have a degree of confidence in it already.

This typical general education writing process method, I believe, misses critical opportunities to impact ELs' literacy skill development that could accelerate their English proficiency from the beginning stages. As a result, I found through experience and observation that by routinely incorporating assets-based EL-specific writing techniques and personalized error correction as teachable moments in writing instruction improve Newcomers' English phonics, spelling, and basic writing skills in as little as four weeks. Eight EL-specific techniques when integrated into the writing process instructional routines will enhance Newcomers' capability to show what they know.

EL techniques are integrated into the steps of the writing process so that you can keep the pace of your literacy instruction as seamless as possible for the whole class. For most Newcomers, copying may be involved at this early writing stage, of course, and that is fine if it is *copying with comprehension*. This means that Newcomers are writing what they want to say and not just copying what the teacher wrote on the board or word wall. That is just practicing handwriting, not writing. By copying with comprehension, Newcomers will more easily and rapidly internalize the English patterns of sounds, words, and phrases of what they wanted to communicate because these thoughts are tied to their emotions, repetition, and/or internal associations (Sousa, 2010). This is how we learn.

Table I.2 shows that the EL Writing Process protocol involves personalized, small group, and whole class dimensions. Subsequent chapters will delve into the details of each EL technique; however, the overview is important for your complete understanding of this integrated process.

Table I.2 EL Writing Process Integration Techniques

EL WRITING PROCESS

Pre-Writing Step	• 1) Level 1 Materials & Tasks • 2) Model Final Product
Writing Step	• 3) Draw to Draft • 4) WORD LINE Tool
Edit & Revise Step	• 5) Teacher Underwriting • 6) Phonics Flexing
Publish Step	• 7) Write to Spell Mini-Lessons • 8) Rewrite for Repetition & Publishing

EL Writing Process

"Change is almost always messy", writes Jim Knight in *The Impact Cycle* (2018, p. 138). Get ready to *slightly yet purposely* change your writing and literacy teaching practices for your Newcomers.

Why You Should Read This Book

Teacher, this book is designed to assist you and your beginner Newcomer in developing foundational literacy skills. If you feel isolated or insecure about your limited experience in teaching Newcomers and beginner ELs English reading and writing skills, you are not alone. Scholars have noted that ESL writing in K-12 contexts has generally been an understudied area (e.g. Hirvela & Belcher, 2007; Matsuda & De Pew, 2002; Ortmeier-Hooper & Enright, 2011). Consequently, there has not been much empirical research on how ESL writing is taught, what challenges teachers encounter, and what strategies can be adopted to overcome these challenges (Bhowmik & Kim, 2021).

Your teacher training program may have included how to teach the writing process to native English speakers; however, few programs include how to teach writing to students who have another language and writing script in their heads. As a result, writing workshop times have proven to be ineffective for ELs across the nation. The National Assessment of Educational Progress (NAEP) reports 65% of eighth-grade ELs performed below basic proficiency in writing, compared to only 17% of eighth-grade proficient native English speakers (NCES, 2012). Hirvela and Belcher (2007) state that "we have tended to focus more of our attention on the needs of those learning to write in a second language rather than of those learning to teach writing" (p. 128). This underscores the importance of this book and your need to seek EL writing teacher training from an experienced teacher of English language acquisition like me.

"These persistent inequalities are, in part, related to the instruction students receive, as many educators report having little to no training in teaching writing" (Gilbert & Graham, 2010). With the increasing numbers of public-school student ELs in the United States rising from 9.2 percent, or 4.6 million students, in fall 2011 to 10.6 percent, or 5.3 million students, in 2021, you most likely will have at least one EL in your class every year (National Center for Educational Statistics, 2024). Many education researchers have criticized the lack of explicit language instruction in the mainstream classroom, arguing that ELs need systemic instruction in academic language to be successful in school (de Jong & Harper, 2005; Dutro & Helman, 2009).

As you read this book and discover how EL techniques are seamlessly woven into your writing instruction activities, you will build your own confidence in teaching writing to Newcomers as they accelerate their own pace of English literacy acquisition. You will also discover how the EL Writing Process protocol affords you the flexibility to adapt to evolving Newcomer needs, and you are not rigidly set to a timeline or prescribed set of curricular materials. You are the expert in your class. This book gives you a systemic roadmap to get your ELs from point A to point B of literacy skills.

To see where you are in terms of readiness for this EL-focused writing instruction challenge in your teaching practice, take the self-efficacy needs assessment on effectively teaching beginner Newcomers phonics, spelling, and writing skills for increased literacy. Based on your results, you will be advised on how to proceed with this book and other additional training throughout your career. Ongoing professional development is a trait of any good, effective teacher like you!

Self-Efficacy Needs Assessment for Teachers of Newcomers in Basic Academic Phonics, Spelling, and Writing

Teaching basic academic phonics, spelling, and writing skills to Newcomer ELs requires specific knowledge and purposeful use of strategies. Teachers like you have varying levels of that specific knowledge and strategies; therefore, you may need to read all or only some parts of this book. Either way, you will take away valuable insights and tools for setting your Newcomers on their way to fluent English writing.

This self-efficacy needs assessment aims to evaluate your confidence level in your ability to effectively teach fundamental skills of phonics, spelling, and basic writing to Newcomer students. By assessing your self-efficacy, you can identify areas where you may need further support and development. This survey is also found in editable form in the Support Materials folder for this book.

Instructions

Please read each statement and rate your confidence level on a scale of 1 – low, 2 – medium, and 3 – high confidence.

1. I feel confident in my ability to teach basic phonics concepts to Newcomer students.
   1 – Low
   2 – Medium
   3 – High
2. I am knowledgeable about effective strategies for teaching spelling to Newcomer students, considering their language proficiency level.
   1 – Low
   2 – Medium
   3 – High
3. I feel confident in my ability to scaffold writing instruction for Newcomer students, helping them develop basic writing skills.
   1 – Low

2 – Medium

3 – High

4. I understand how to differentiate instructions in phonics, spelling, and writing to meet the diverse needs of Newcomer students.

   1 – Low

   2 – Medium

   3 – High

5. I am comfortable assessing Newcomer students' progress in phonics, spelling, and writing and using assessment data to inform my instruction.

   1 – Low

   2 – Medium

   3 – High

6. I feel confident in my ability to create engaging and culturally responsive learning activities for teaching phonics, spelling, and writing to Newcomer students.

   1 – Low

   2 – Medium

   3 – High

7. I actively seek out professional development opportunities to enhance my understanding of teaching phonics, spelling, and writing to Newcomer students.

   1 – Low

   2 – Medium

   3 – High

8. I understand the importance of providing explicit instruction and ample practice opportunities in phonics, spelling, and writing for Newcomer students to build their skills effectively.

   1 – Low

   2 – Medium

   3 – High

9. I feel confident in my ability to support Newcomer students who may have limited prior literacy experiences in their native language.

   1 – Low

   2 – Medium

   3 – High

10. Overall, I feel confident in my ability to teach basic academic phonics, spelling, and writing skills to Newcomer students.
    1 – Low
    2 – Medium
    3 – High

Total: Number of each score _____ x 1s + _____ x 2s + _____ x 3s = Total Score _____ /30 possible points

Reflection

After completing the assessment, take a moment to reflect on your responses. Identify any areas where you rated yourself lower and consider how you can further develop your knowledge and skills in those areas. In addition, acknowledge areas where you feel confident and consider how you can leverage those strengths to support your Newcomer students effectively. Remember, continuous learning and reflection are essential for professional growth as an educator.

Overall Rating Scale

The scale of 1 to 30 indicates your preferred approach for enhancing your teaching skills in basic academic phonics, spelling, and writing for Newcomer students. Please choose one option that best reflects your needs:

1–10: In Need of Understanding More and Building My Confidence in Literacy Teaching!
  • I prefer to read this book from cover to cover to gain a comprehensive understanding of language acquisition concepts and EL-centered literacy techniques. Start with reading Part 1 before tackling the EL Writing Process techniques.
  • I would benefit from in-person training to reinforce my understanding and receive direct feedback on my teaching practice.
11–20: Somewhat Confident in How to Teach Literacy to Newcomers but Still Learning!
  • I am willing to read this book cover to cover to grasp the fundamental concepts and strategies thoroughly. Start by skimming

through Part 1 to refresh your memory of language acquisition and literacy learning.

- I feel comfortable with self-paced, how-to learn asynchronous courses but may seek additional resources or support from experienced EL writing teachers as needed.

21–30: I am Confident Teaching Newcomers, but Literacy Instruction Baffles Me!

- I will skim through Part 1 of the book to understand the foundational principles of this EL Writing Process protocol and then jump to Part 2. OR

I prefer to dive directly into Part 2 to learn the practical techniques and strategies for teaching phonics, spelling, and writing to Newcomer students.

References

Berninger, V. W., & Winn, W. D. (2006). Implications of advancements in brain research and technology for writing development, writing instruction, and educational evolution. In C. A. MacArthur, S. Graham, & J. Fitzgerald (Eds.), *Handbook of writing research* (pp. 96–114). Guilford Press.

Bhowmik, S., & Kim, M. (2021). K-12 ESL writing instruction: A review of research on pedagogical challenges and strategies. *Language and Literacy, 23*(3), 165–189.

de Jong, E., & Harper, C. (2005). Preparing mainstream teachers for English-language learners: Is being a good teacher good enough? *Teacher Education Quarterly, 32*(2), 101–124.

Dutro, S., & Helman, L. A. (2009). Explicit language instruction: A key to constructing meaning: Research-based instruction in grades K-6. In L. A. Helman (Ed.), *Literacy development with English learners: Research-based instruction in grades K-6* (pp. 40–63). Guilford Press.

Flower, L. S., & Hayes, J. R. (1981). A cognitive process theory of writing. *College Composition & Communication, 32*(4), 365–387.

Gilbert, J., & Graham, S. (2010). Teaching writing to elementary students in grades 4–6: A national survey. *The Elementary School Journal, 110*(4), 494–518.

Greenwald, E. A., Persky, H. R., Campbell, J. R., & Mazzeo, J. (1999). *NAEP 1998 writing: Report card for the nation and the states.* National Centre for Education Statistics.

Hirvela, A., & Belcher, D. (2007). Writing scholars as teacher educators: Exploring writing teacher education. *Journal of Second Language Writing, 16*(3), 125–128.

Knight, J. (2018). *The impact cycle: what instructional coaches should do to foster powerful improvements in teaching*. Corwin, A Sage Company.

Matsuda, P. K., & De Pew, K. E. (2002). Early second language writing: An introduction. *Journal of Second Language Writing, 11*(4), 261–268.

McCullough, D. (2002, July–August). Interview with NEH chairman Bruce Cole. *Humanities, 23*(4).

National Center for Education Statistics. (2012). *The nation's report card: Writing 2011 (NCES 2012-470)*. U.S. Department of Education, Institute of Education Sciences. https://nces.ed.gov/nationsreportcard/pubs/main2011/2012470.asp

National Center for Education Statistics (NCES). (2024). *English learners in public schools. Condition of education*. U.S. Department of Education, Institute of Education Sciences. https://nces.ed.gov/programs/coe/indicator/cgf

Ortmeier-Hooper, C., & Enright, K. A. (2011). Mapping new territory: Toward as understanding of adolescent L2 writers and writing in US contexts. *Journal of Second Language Writing, 20*(3), 167–181.

Pugh, K. R., Mencl, W. E., Jenner, A. R., Lee, J. R., Katz, L., Frost, S. J., Shaywitz, S. E., & Shaywitz, B. A. (2001). Neuroimaging studies of reading development and reading disability. *Learning Disabilities Research & Practice, 16*(4), 240–249.

Sousa, D. A. (2010). *How the ell brain learns*. Corwin Press.

Unger, J. R., & Fleischman, S. (2004). Is process writing the 'write stuff'? *Educational Leadership, 62*, 90–91.

PART 1

Basics of Language Acquisition and the Needs of Newcomers

1 Who Are English Learner Newcomers?

Eugenia Krimmel

Newcomers are part of a larger group of bilingual students. Multilingual learners (MLs) is a broad term for U.S. school-aged students who know and function in languages other than English while learning academic content and skills. This group consists of currently identified English learners (ELs), never-EL heritage speakers, and former English learners (FELs) who completed the ELD program while in K12 school. These students all have at least one other language system in their heads through social and/or academic circumstances. MLs have a larger linguistic repertoire of phonemes and grammar than their monolingual peers, bringing more linguistic knowledge to their academic English writing development. Teachers are advised to provide opportunities for all MLs to use the assets they bring to literacy learning.

How Do We Identify an English Learner?

The process to determine if a student is an EL or not begins with the home language survey that is required of all families to complete as part of the enrollment paperwork for U.S. public schools (U.S. Department of Education, Office of English Language Acquisition, 2017). Private schools are not required to provide home language surveys, but they can. This survey asks if a language other than English is used at home. If yes, the student or students in the family are placed on a list for further investigation as to their language needs. In some states like Pennsylvania, the school or district must follow up with a family interview to learn whether

DOI: 10.4324/9781003610595-3

the language used at home could hinder learning in English at school (Pennsylvania Department of Education, 2023). These interview questions ask about how often a child hears and speaks the home language, who speaks the home language, and to what degree: occasionally, sometimes, always, or never does the child use the language. The purpose of this family interview is to avoid unnecessary testing. For example, if a family says Greek or Hebrew is spoken at home in the home language survey, then technically those students are to be tested for language needs. However, if the children at home are learning Greek or Hebrew in Saturday school for cultural or religious purposes, then those languages are not spoken often enough to become barriers to learning in an English-speaking school; therefore, these students do not continue in the EL identification process as required by some state and federal mandates.

Standardized statewide English language proficiency (ELP) screeners are federally required for the next step in determining if a child is an EL or not (U.S. Department of Education, Office of English Language Acquisition, 2017). The criteria, however, for in or out of this EL status is set by each state. Students who exceed the cut-off for being "in" EL status are not considered ELs and are labeled never-ELs. Students whose scores on the English language skills screener assessment fall short of the cut-off score are considered ELs until they meet the exit criteria on annual proficiency testing. Some states developed their own assessments and aligned scales of ELP, while others joined a consortium using shared systems such as:

ELPA21 – English Language Proficiency Assessment for the 21st Century Consortium
WIDA – World-Class Instructional Design and Assessment Consortium

Each ELP system marks a line or level on their scales determining which students are in or out of the ELD school program based on their test results. These screener test results become official documents for identification and each student qualifying will be reported to their respective state's department of education for federal reporting and funding. Each language proficiency scale has ELP-level numbers and word labels.

For example, the ELPA21 (2020) uses a scale of labeled levels: (Level 1) Beginning, (Level 2) Early Intermediate, (Level 3) Intermediate, and (Level 4) Early Advanced. The WIDA Consortium uses a similar scale based on their assessment tools with slightly different labels: Level (1) Entering Level (2) Emerging Level (3) Developing Level (4) Expanding Level (5) Bridging Level and (6) Reaching (WIDA, 2020). States such as California, New York, and Texas, among others, have created their own screening and annual proficiency assessments; therefore, they use their own unique scales. Each test measures proficiency by language skill (listening, reading, speaking, and writing) and combines those scores for a single proficiency level. Because proficiency levels are a composite of the four language skill scores combined, writing may not be as strong for some ELs even in more advanced stages.

Language Development versus Language Proficiency

Educational researchers contend that *language development* is a learner's capabilities at a given moment along the language learning continuum whereas *language proficiency* is a broader concept of language levels meant to group students within a program (Wolfe-Quintero et al., 1998; Manchon, 2012). For this reason, ELs' writing skills may be lower on the scale than their overall level of English proficiency. An intermediate-level EL may perform at a beginner EL writing level for a variety of reasons: lack of writing opportunities, struggles with English spelling and writing patterns, or little motivation to write in English.

As you can see, not all MLs are ELs, but all ELs are bilingual learners or MLs who have to function academically in more than one language. ELs bring linguistic assets to every class experience from day one. Their funds of knowledge contribute to their ability to communicate and learn an additional language. We celebrate what ELs produce in English while valuing their first language attributes that form the basis of their individual literacy skills.

Who Are Newcomers and Beginner English Learners?

In U.S. public schools, 85% of grades K–5 ELs and 62% of grade 6–12 ELs are born in one of the 50 U.S. states (Zong & Batalova, 2015); however,

ELs also come from outside the country and are known as Newcomers. According to the U.S. Department of Education and the National Clearinghouse for English Language Acquisition (NCELA) Newcomer Toolkit, "Newcomers are defined as K-12 students born outside the United States who have arrived in the country in the last three years and are still learning English" (June, 2023, p. 8). The toolkit definition also states the term *Newcomer* is used as an umbrella term for students and their families who have come to the United States voluntarily as opposed to other new arrivals who have fled as refugees and/or those students with interrupted schooling.

Newcomer immigrant students with interrupted schooling are known as *Students with Limited or Interrupted Formal Education* (SLIFE) or in some states, they are known as *Students with Interrupted Formal Education* (SIFE). According to the Virginia Department of Education (2020), a SLIFE student is

> an English learner who enters or re-enters any school in the United States at or after the age of eight and is identified at English Language Proficiency (ELP) Level one or two and has at least two years less schooling than similar-age peers.

Despite lacking academic skills, SLIFE students often have a wealth of experience to bring to classroom discussions (Lindahl, 2015). They come from heterogeneous backgrounds and contexts quite different from U.S. schooling (DeCapua & Marshall, 2011) and may have been subject to migration, war, or placement in refugee camps, among other life challenges (Custodio & O'Loughlin, 2017). Research suggests that the majority of SLIFE students who were tested are still developing word-level decoding skills in English after one year (Klein & Martohardjono, 1999).

Not all Newcomers are beginner ELs. Figure 1.1 reflects the categories of Newcomers. Some may have attended English-based schools in refugee camps, in private or public schools in their home countries, or took years of English classes before coming to the United States. For that reason, we cannot say all Newcomers are beginners or level 1 ELs; however, the majority of Newcomers will initially test into the beginning stages of ELD. In addition to some or little English language learning, Newcomers may have experienced interrupted or no schooling based on factors

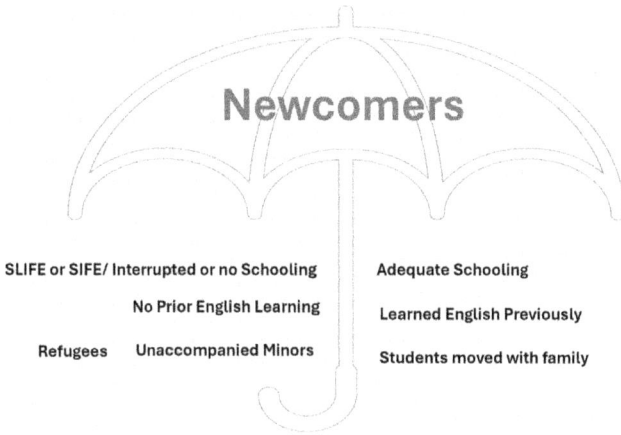

Figure 1.1 Not all newcomers are the same
Source: Created by Eugenia Krimmel, 2024.

such as gender, poverty, and social disruptions of war or natural causes. Because Newcomers were born outside the United States, some come with their families but others do not, which may contribute to emotional factors in their learning journey.

The focus of this book is on Newcomers who are at the entering or beginning level of academic language learning. This often includes SIFE/SLIFE students and those with little to no prior English learning of all ages. We are tasked with teaching every genius who enters our schools and classrooms. It will be tough at times, but through a systematic process of teaching the integrated EL techniques, you will accelerate Newcomers' learning for future success.

Impact of Parents' Lack of English Proficiency

As an ELD instructional coach, I am often asked if a student is an EL based on the fact their parents speak little to no English. The answer is an obvious "no". Parents may not have had exposure or opportunity to learn English in their younger years, but the children may have. You must approach each Newcomer's instruction based on the evidence we have of their funds of knowledge and not those of parents or siblings. Screener testing, while helpful, does not tell us everything about the language needs of individual students. You must observe, listen, and try various strategies that allow students to show what they know. Only then will you have a fuller picture of what an EL, a Newcomer, can receive or produce in academic English.

Reflection Questions:

1. To identify students as ELs, what is the process required from the federal mandates to state regulations where you are a current teacher or learning as a pre-service teacher?
2. What are the various distinctions among Newcomer ELs and how are their needs different?
3. What are the challenges of teaching literacy skills to Newcomers in our schools today? List each and brainstorm ways to overcome each challenge.

References

Custodio, B., & O'Loughlin, J. (2017). *Students with interrupted formal education: Bridging where they are and what they need.* Corwin.

DeCapua, A., & Marshall, H. W. (2011). Reaching ELLs at risk: Instruction for students with limited or interrupted formal education. *Preventing School Failure: Alternative Education for Children and Youth, 55*(1), 35–41.

Klein, E. C., & Martohardjono, G. (1999). *The development of second language grammars: A generative approach.* J. Benjamins.

Lindahl, K. (2015, November 2). *Tap into funds of knowledge.* http://blog.tesol.org/tap-into-funds-of-knowledge/

Manchon, R. M. (Ed.). (2012). *L2 writing development: Multiple perspectives.* Walter de Gruyter.

Pennsylvania Department of Education. (2023). *English learner identification procedure grades K-12.* Screening, Identification, and Placement of ELs. https://www.pa.gov/agencies/education/programs-and-services/instruction/elementary-and-secondary-education/curriculum/educating-english-learners/screening-identification-and-placement.html

U.S. Department of Education, & National Clearinghouse for English Language Acquisition (NCELA). (2023). *Newcomer toolkit.* https://ncela.ed.gov/sites/default/files/2023-09/NewcomerToolkit-09152023-508.pdf

U.S. Department of Education, Office of English Language Acquisition. (2017). *English learner tool kit* (2nd Rev. ed.). Author.

Virginia Department of Education. (2020). *Students with limited and/or interrupted formal education guidebook.* https://doe.virginia.gov/instruction/esl/resources/slife-guidebook.pdf

WIDA. (2020). *WIDA English language development standards framework, 2020 edition: Kindergarten–grade 12.* Board of Regents of the University of Wisconsin System.

Wolfe-Quintero, K., Inagaki, S., & Kim, H. Y. (1998). *Second language development in writing: Measures of fluency, accuracy and complexity.* Second Language Teaching & Curriculum Center, University of Hawai'i.

Zong, J., & Batalova, J. (2015). *The limited English proficient population in the United States.* Migration Policy.

Crash Course in Second Language Acquisition Stages

Stages of Second Language Proficiency

Understanding the second language learning continuum helps you understand your ELs including your Newcomers as they progress along the continuum of language acquisition stages. SLA is a complex process through which individuals learn a new language in addition to their native language(s). Moving through the stages of SLA can vary depending on factors such as age, exposure, motivation, and individual differences. However, researchers have identified several common stages (see Table 2.1) that learners typically go through when acquiring a second language.

The level labels tell you very little about what the bilingual brain is experiencing at each stage. Researchers like Krashen and Terrell (1983) have described each stage in more detail:

1. Preproduction (silent period)
   - During this stage, learners may be silent as they observe the new language in use.
   - They have an extremely limited vocabulary of 1–50 words approximately.
   - They are actively absorbing the new language through listening and observation.
2. Early Production
   - In this stage, learners begin to produce a few familiar words and short phrases in the new language.

DOI: 10.4324/9781003610595-4

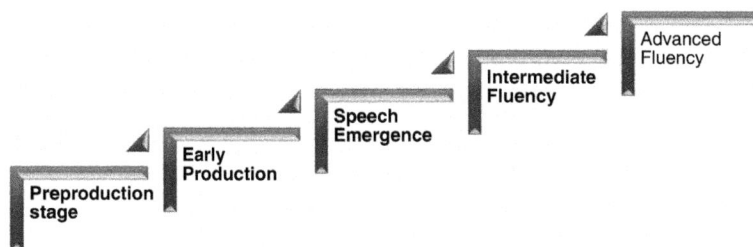

Advanced Fluency

Intermediate Fluency

Speech Emergence

Early Production

Preproduction stage

Table 2.1 Stages of Second Language Acquisition

Source: Adapted from Krashen and Terrell (1983).

- They may use simple, high-frequency vocabulary and basic sentence structures.
- Their language production contains errors, but they are starting to communicate in the target language.

3. Speech Emergence
   - Learners in this stage can produce more complex sentences and express themselves more fluently with fewer errors.
   - They start to understand and use grammar rules more accurately.
   - Vocabulary expands, allowing them to convey a wider range of ideas in the new language.

4. Intermediate Fluency
   - At this stage, learners have a good grasp of the language patterns and can engage in conversations with greater ease.
   - They demonstrate the ability to learn and express complex linguistic structures and broader vocabulary to independently communicate in academic English settings.
   - While they still make a few errors, they are able to communicate effectively in most situations.

5. Advanced Fluency
   - They can understand and express themselves with near-peer fluency.
   - Their vocabulary is extensive, and they can communicate effectively in both informal and formal academic contexts.
   - They may still have a slight accent or occasional errors, but overall, their language skills are highly proficient.

It is important to note that these stages are not rigid and linear; learners may move back and forth between stages, and the process of SLA is highly individualized. Additionally, external factors such as motivation, exposure to the language, and opportunities for practice can significantly influence the speed and effectiveness of language acquisition.

What Do ELP Levels Mean?

Identifying ELs in grades K–12 of U.S. public schools requires understanding how ELP proficiency levels align with SLA stages. Here is a summary of how these stages and levels correlate to help you better understand the documentation you read about each EL in your school. Because some states use their own scale labels and other states joined a consortium using other labels, this book includes the most widely known scale produced by the WIDA Consortium, a research organization that supports educators of MLs by offering standards, assessments, instructional resources, and professional development opportunities. ELP levels are aligned to the SLA stages that are designed for anyone learning a new or additional language.

Teachers have asked me if Level 1 meant the top or most proficient and Level 5 was the lower and more basic level. These teachers referred to Level 1 as they would in the MTSS model of Tier 1 representing students

Table 2.2 English Language Proficiency Scale

Levels of English Language Proficiency					**Level 6**
				Level 5	Reaching
			Level 4	Bridging	
		Level 3	Expanding		
	Level 2	Developing			
Level 1	Emerging				
Entering					

Source: Based on WIDA ELD 2020 Standards Framework (WIDA, 2020).

with the least need for special instruction. Why are these levels important for your teaching, you may ask. By modifying and differentiating your instruction to these levels, educators can scaffold ELs' growth effectively by supporting their progress to the reaching level of English proficiency. Table 2.2 gives you an at-a-glance review of the ELP proficiency chart which starts with Level 1 as the most basic.

English Language Proficiency Levels Aligned to SLA Stages

1. Preproduction/Silent Period (ESL Level 1 – Entering)
   In this initial stage, students primarily listen without speaking much. Level 1 ELs understand basic language with visual support but may not be able to speak fluently or produce complex sentences. Instruction focuses on simple commands and visuals.
2. Early Production (ESL Level 2 – Emerging or Beginning)
   At this stage, ELs begin to respond with short phrases. Level 2 students build basic vocabulary and benefit from sentence starters and guided responses to encourage language use.
3. Speech Emergence (ESL Level 3 – Developing)
   Students at this level communicate basic ideas and hold simple conversations. Level 3 ELs can construct sentences but still need support for language complexity, such as structured discussions and sentence expansion.
4. Intermediate Fluency (ESL Level 4 – Expanding)
   ELs at this level demonstrate more fluent language use, with stronger vocabulary and sentence structure. Level 4 students engage in academic discourse with some grammatical accuracy and benefit from lessons that deepen comprehension and critical thinking.
5. Advanced Fluency (ESL Level 5 – Bridging)
   At this stage, students' language skills are nearly on par with native speakers. Level 5 ELs may need occasional academic language support but are largely independent and can handle complex tasks with minimal assistance.

Designated versus Integrated ELD Instructional Program Models

Identified ELs from Level 1 to Level 4 proficiency must receive language assistance. How that assistance is designed plays a role within the school for standards alignment, credits, and other considerations. This book addresses writing instruction in either integrated or designated ELD program models.

Content-integrated ELD occurs when content teachers use language modifications and scaffolds to enhance Newcomer's comprehension of grade-level curriculum and resources which are often not Level 1 appropriate for comprehension. Content teachers *teach content through the language* of their subject. Designated ELD instruction separates ELD instructional time when ESL teachers teach *language skills through content* to ELs in a school's ELD program (Wolf-Greenberg et al., 2022).

The EL Writing Process will become a natural part of your writing workshop practice whether you teach in an integrated setting with ELs and non-ELs targeting your Newcomers as needed or in a designated program with only Newcomers who are encountering English for the first time. The goal is to give you as the teacher of Newcomers a systematic approach to teaching structured literacy to ELs in grades 3–12 in which the curriculum does not typically involve phonology, phonics, and spelling within the writing instruction.

Integrated Skill Development for English Learners

Language skills (listening, speaking, reading, and writing) combine sets of complex subskills. Table 2.3 shows a simplified version of two subskills per language skill to illustrate what is involved in developing these interpretive and expressive skills for a student's first or additional language acquisition. Each subskill can be broken into even more micro-skills not shown in this table. Note that each skill requires comprehension or the ability to communicate comprehensibly to be fully proficient in language.

Table 2.3 Language Skills and Subskills

Listening	Deciphering phonemes into sounds, words, and sentences	Comprehension of oral sensory information in the new language system
Speaking	Pronunciation of new language sounds and sound patterns to speak	Comprehensibility in spoken communication of one's thoughts in grammatically correct utterances
Reading	Decoding individual letters to sounds within words, word combinations, intonation, and fluency (word recognition)	Comprehension of contextual reading passages for learning information
Writing	Handwriting, letter/word formation, encoding/spelling of words to convey the meaning of one's thoughts	Comprehensibility in written communication of one's thoughts in grammatically correct words, phrases, sentences, and longer text

Oral Language Skills' Impact on Newcomer Literacy Skill Development

The key to teaching literacy skills to Newcomers is developing oral language skills through listening and speaking interaction in classroom activities. Newcomers will gradually internalize English phonology (sounds), morphology (word parts), semantics (word meaning), and syntax (grammar) patterns with time and exposure to academic English in engaging ways. English, however, is a low-correspondence language meaning that one sound is represented by more than one letter, and one letter may have multiple sounds such as "a" in *hat, saw, was, watch, and April*. Spanish and Turkish, for example, are high-correspondence languages that have one-sound-one letter correlation. Because English has such complex decoding and encoding systems, native and non-native English speakers require years of literacy instruction to navigate this beautifully complicated language. Table 2.4 illustrates the subskills of listening and speaking.

Table 2.4 Subskills or Components of Oral Language

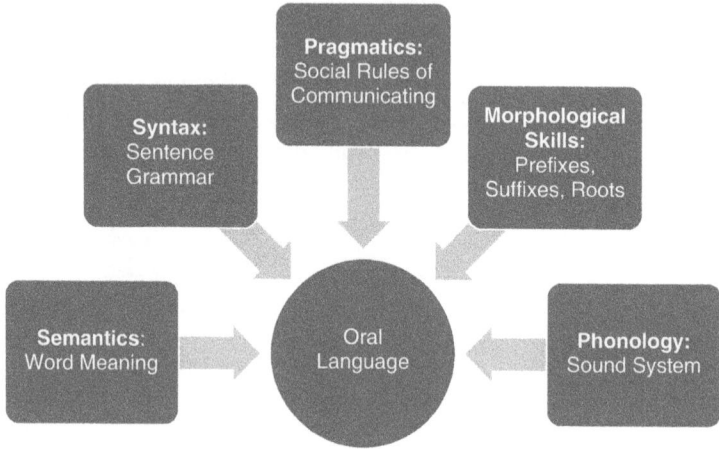

Source: Created by Eugenia Krimmel, 2025.

Your teaching practice for Newcomers must routinely include listening and speaking activities at their basic linguistic level using lots of gestures, visuals, and realia: physical objects representing something like a toy car for a real car or an elephant statue instead of a real elephant. Opportunities for instructional conversations around learning will contribute greatly to all students learning. I have seen too many Newcomers sitting in a corner or not encouraged to participate in oral language activities. Some teachers argue they do not want to force an EL in their silent period to talk. This "silent period" of three to six months is when an entering EL is taking in the new language sounds but cannot produce those sounds on their own, yet. Engagement at this very early stage is crucial for language acquisition, serving as both a model and input for the bilingual brain to begin making associations. Involve Newcomers in listening and speaking at all times.

Reading Skill Development for Newcomers

The National Reading Panel Report (2000) commissioned by the National Institute of Child Health and Human claims years of scientific research on teaching and learning reading clearly show that literacy instruction must address these five components or pillars:

- Phonemic awareness
- Phonics
- Fluency
- Vocabulary
- Comprehension

The National Literacy Panel on Language-Minority Children and Youth emphasizes that ELLs require scaffolded instruction to develop English literacy skills (August & Shanahan, 2006). Their comprehensive report, released in 2006, highlights the urgent challenge for teachers to teach ELs literacy effectively and it underscores the unique needs of ELs in acquiring reading and writing skills.

Reading Skill Development for ELs

As renowned literacy expert Louisa Moats asserts, "The Science of Reading is not a method; it's a body of knowledge based on decades of scientific research on reading and spelling processes" (2020). The Science of Reading's culminating evidence of effective literacy instruction serves as a critical foundation for you to better understand what to teach your Newcomers and why. Drawing on the evidence-based practices of explicitly teaching Newcomers phonemic awareness, phonics, fluency, vocabulary, and comprehension while fostering oral language skills, acknowledging cultural relevance, and building on background knowledge of writing workshop topics is the big picture of the EL Writing Process protocol.

What Is the EL Writing Process?

The EL Writing Process is a method of integrating the teaching of foundational literacy skills to non-native English speakers. For teaching English as an additional language, you can look to the knowledge and skill development of the Science of Reading principles because these aspects resonate

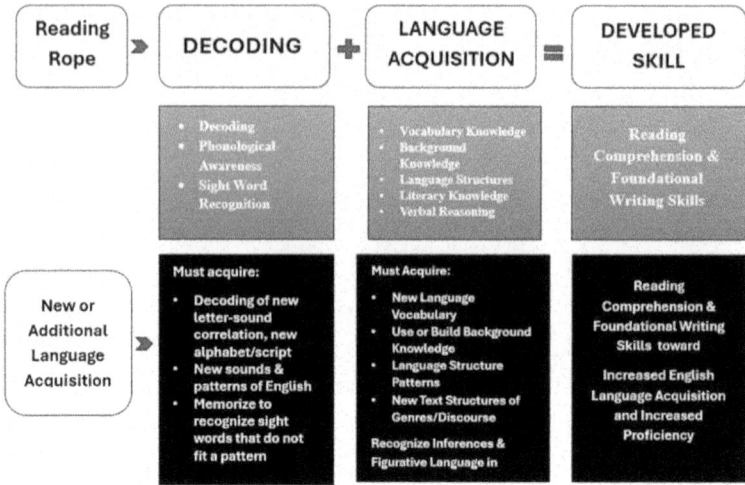

Reading Rope ➤	DECODING	➕	LANGUAGE ACQUISITION	＝	DEVELOPED SKILL
	• Decoding • Phonological Awareness • Sight Word Recognition		• Vocabulary Knowledge • Background Knowledge • Language Structures • Literacy Knowledge • Verbal Reasoning		Reading Comprehension & Foundational Writing Skills
New or Additional Language Acquisition ➤	**Must acquire:** • Decoding of new letter-sound correlation, new alphabet/script • New sounds & patterns of English • Memorize to recognize sight words that do not fit a pattern		**Must Acquire:** • New Language Vocabulary • Use or Build Background Knowledge • Language Structure Patterns • New Text Structures of Genres/Discourse Recognize Inferences & Figurative Language in		Reading Comprehension & Foundational Writing Skills toward Increased English Language Acquisition and Increased Proficiency

Figure 2.1 Reading Rope aligned to language acquisition

Source: Created by E. Krimmel, 2025. Adapted from Scarborough, H. S. (2001). Connecting early language and literacy to later reading (dis)abilities: Evidence, theory, and practice. In S. Neuman & D. Dickinson (Eds.), *Handbook for research in early literacy* (pp. 97–110). Guilford Press.

with the cognitive processes of language acquisition. Illustrated in the Science of Reading underpinnings from Scarborough's Reading Rope (2001) (Figure 2.1) you can clearly see how foundational skills in developing literacy correlate with initial language acquisition steps. By integrating these principles into writing instruction, you foster Newcomers' decoding and encoding abilities and in turn facilitate language acquisition toward increased writing fluency, linguistic confidence, and academic English success.

To effectively provide personalized feedback and literacy instruction for your Newcomers to establish their foundational literacy skills, you must acquire a degree of expertise in teaching phonics and spelling. Most teachers surveyed do not feel they know the alphabetic code, morphology, and other linguistic rules of English to effectively teach students decoding and encoding skills (Treiman, 2018). How can anyone teach something they do not know?

Professional development programs grounded in the Science of Reading equip educators with structured literacy knowledge and purposeful strategies necessary to impart phonics and spelling skills to all students, especially Newcomers. By understanding the cognitive processes involved in reading and writing, you implement targeted, personalized feedback tailored to individual student needs. This knowledge enables you to identify specific areas of challenge and address Newcomers' unique linguistic needs. Embracing the Science of Reading as part of your ongoing professional learning opportunities not only enhances your instructional efficacy but also contributes to a more inclusive and equitable learning environment in which all your students, ELs and non-ELs, can thrive in developing their English literacy skills.

Scarborough's Reading Rope (2001) illustrates all the elements of the reading skill necessary to master the written symbols of a language with understanding. Note how both aspects of reading, that is, decoding and language comprehension, require effective, systematic literacy instruction. Some upper elementary to high school teachers whom I observed jump right into the language comprehension tasks because those match grade-level content standards; however, students may also need more decoding skill development. Newcomers at beginning proficiency levels definitely need instruction and practice in all literacy skills; therefore, you must find time to address those needs within your instructional practice.

Too often I observed teachers making assumptions that ELs who properly decode words understand what they read. I call these ELs "word callers". Good decoding skills can lead to increased comprehension, but it does not cause comprehension. The EL Writing Process approaches literacy instruction for Newcomers from both views of reading: decoding and language comprehension. Using mostly their own words or those taught during pre-writing, Newcomers understand what they are writing. During teacher underwriting (TU) and phonics flexing (PF) they learn decoding and spelling.

Structured Literacy for ELs in a Nutshell

Most of you have heard this educational term, "structured literacy". You may understand the principles and applications for native English-speaking students, but how does it differ for students who have another language in their heads? How does literacy development vary for Newcomers in grades 3–12 within the new push for structured literacy in all grades and content? Some researchers are trying to convince teachers that structured literacy is not different for ELs, yet how can that be without internalized patterns of English to rely on when reading and writing?

From Table 2.5 you can see how all the elements of structured literacy are part of the overall reading and writing skill; however, these are based on internalization of English patterns in one's brain. Newcomers have a different set of patterns in their brains, so those new to English will need more explicit teaching, more repetition, and more need for practice to achieve automaticity in both oral and written communication.

Structured literacy is an educational approach that is explicit, systematic, and sequential to teaching elements of literacy based on oral language knowledge. The pendulum of educational approaches from whole language to phonics and back again has currently settled on instruction that focuses on teaching the foundational skills of reading, including phonological awareness, phonics, spelling, grammar, and comprehension strategies. The components of structured literacy for ELs expose the reasons why the phonics-focused approach is particularly beneficial for beginning ELs, especially Newcomers.

Table 2.5 Elements of Structured Literacy

Phonology	Sound to Symbol	Syllable Instruction
		el/ e/ phant elephant
Morphology	**Semantics**	**Syntax**
Un **comfort** able Prefix root suffix		Mike reads a book. Subject + verb + article + object.

Components of Structured Literacy Teaching for ELs

1. **Explicit Instruction**: This involves direct teaching of concepts with clear and concise explanations and linguistic rules. Students do not have to infer literacy concepts on their own.
2. **Systematic and Sequential**: Instruction follows a logical order, starting with the simplest and most fundamental concepts and gradually progressing to more complex skills. Although language is not learned sequentially, instruction is typically presented in a simple-to-complex progression.
3. **Phonological Awareness:** Teaching students to recognize and manipulate the sounds of the spoken English language is critical for reading and writing development. Newcomers have other language patterns in their heads that they will refer to often in the beginning. Purposeful phonological awareness activities help them acquire English as a new linguistic code in their minds which, in turn, assists their literacy acquisition.
4. **Phonics**: Instruction on the relationship between letters and sounds enables students to decode and encode or spell words. Learning letter-sound correlation is a typical stumbling block most Newcomers encounter unless effective phonics instruction helps them learn. Now that structured literacy practices will be in place in schools in Pennsylvania and other states, including secondary grades, this challenge will be addressed for most ELs.
5. **Spelling**: Teaching the rules and patterns of spelling to support reading and writing. Newcomers benefit from explicit teaching of spelling rules, rulebreakers (aka sight words), and pronunciation norms.
6. **Vocabulary**: Expanding students' knowledge of vocabulary improves comprehension and expression. Structured literacy instruction is not complete without comprehension activities and practice. Newcomers may know what a concept is in their native language, but they need the English word for it to learn and express what they know.
7. **Fluency**: Developing the ability to read with speed, accuracy, and proper expression leads to automatic decoding, but it does not guarantee comprehension. Some ELs are good "word callers" who broke

the code of English, but they understand little of what they read aloud. Fluency is a goal for more advanced ELs, but for Newcomers, the priority is learning English patterns.

8. **Comprehension Strategies**: Teaching methods to understand, remember, and communicate what is read involves morphology such as learning the use and meaning of prefixes, word roots, and suffixes. Beyond this, figurative language, text structures, and genres are all important elements of effective structured literacy instruction.

How Does Structured Literacy Instruction Teach Newcomers Reading and Writing?

1. **Clear and Direct Instruction**: Newcomers benefit from explicit teaching because it leaves less room for misunderstandings, ensuring they grasp foundational skills of reading and writing effectively.

2. **Building Strong Foundations**: By systematically building from simple to complex skills, ELs can develop a solid understanding of the English patterns, which is crucial for their academic reading and writing proficiency.

3. **Focus on Phonological Awareness and Phonics:** Many ELs may come from language backgrounds with different phonetic systems. Structured literacy helps them learn the specific sounds and spelling rules of English, which aids in accurate reading and pronunciation for curricular success.

4. **Multisensory Techniques:** Structured literacy often uses multisensory instruction (visual, auditory, and kinesthetic/tactile) which can enhance memory and learning, particularly beneficial for students with diverse learning needs and backgrounds.

5. **Incremental Progression:** The sequential nature of structured literacy assists Newcomers in building their skills gradually, reducing the cognitive load and preventing them from becoming overwhelmed. Although language learning is not linear, sequential learning enhances the brain's process of attaching new input to familiar concepts.

6. **Assessment and Differentiation**: Regular assessment helps identify areas where Newcomers may need additional support. Instruction can then be tailored to meet their specific needs, ensuring that no student falls behind.

7. **Improved Spelling and Writing:** Structured literacy's focus on spelling rules and patterns encourages Newcomers to write more accurately and confidently, reinforcing their reading skills.

8. **Enhanced Vocabulary and Comprehension:** Explicit vocabulary instruction and comprehension strategies ensure that Newcomers not only read fluently but also understand and engage with the content they read.

Structured literacy is particularly crucial for all ELs in grades 3–12, when the curriculum often assumes foundational literacy skills are already in place. In these upper grades, structured literacy becomes a lifeline, providing Newcomers with the supportive framework they need to catch up and succeed academically. Through systematic teaching of sound-symbol relationships, morphology, syntax, and semantics, structured literacy equips ELs with the tools to decode, comprehend, and express themselves in English. It addresses the gaps left by curricula that may not cater to the needs of ELs, ensuring that they have the foundational literacy skills necessary for academic achievement and future success.

Explicit Instruction versus Discovery Learning for Newcomers

Archer & Hughes Archer, experts in literacy education, emphasize the critical importance of explicit instruction in literacy, particularly for all EL and non-EL students (2011). Archer argues that while discovery learning has its place, it is insufficient for teaching the complex skills required for literacy acquisition of novice learners to any concept, whereas those with more foundational knowledge and skills of a concept may benefit from discovery learning. Table 2.6 illustrates this concept for you to differentiate your instructional design and delivery.

In her research, Dr. Archer stresses that explicit instruction provides clear explanations, modeling, and guided practice, which are essential for ELs who may not have exposure to English literacy skills outside of the classroom. She highlights the need for explicit instruction that enables teachers to address the diverse needs of learners, including Newcomers, by breaking down complex skills into manageable components and

Table 2.6 Design of Instruction Continuum

Explicit Instruction	versus	Discovery Learning
Novice learner to concept or skill development		**Some experience of a good foundational knowledge of a skill**

Source: Created by Eugenia Krimmel (2025) based on the work of Anita Archer and Hughes (2011).

providing systematic support like leveled materials and simplified organizers. Archer's work underscores the necessity of structured and explicit literacy instruction to ensure that all students have the foundational skills needed for academic success (Archer & Hughes, 2011). By providing clear instruction and ample opportunities for practice and reinforcement, educators can empower Newcomers to become proficient readers and writers over time, regardless of their language background or previous literacy experiences.

Archer's research delves into the nuanced relationship between the *design* and *delivery* of instruction in literacy teaching. While instructional design focuses on the planning and organization of lessons, instructional delivery encompasses the actual implementation of those plans in the classroom. Archer emphasizes that both aspects are equally crucial for effective literacy instruction. However, she argues that while a well-designed lesson provides a solid framework for learning, its effectiveness ultimately hinges on how it is delivered to students. She advocates for explicit and systematic delivery methods that engage students, provide clear explanations, model desired skills, and offer guided practice opportunities.

Archer underscores the importance of instructional delivery techniques such as direct [accessible] instruction, explicit modeling, and gradual release of responsibility toward discovery learning. By focusing on both the design and delivery of instruction, educators can ensure that literacy instruction is not only well-planned but also effectively implemented to meet the diverse needs of all learners (Archer & Hughes, 2011). When you design and deliver EL Writing Process lessons, you provide such impactful phonics, spelling, and writing instruction as Archer describes.

Developing Writing Skills for English Learners

Writing is as complex a task to teach as it is to learn. Converting one's thoughts into symbols for others to understand and interpret can be a challenging task in one's first language. Imagine the daunting task of learning how to write your thoughts in a language system other than your own inner speech. I often ask Newcomers which language they use to talk to themselves in their heads. I give them the example of how I think in English to myself, but I can speak in other languages. Newcomers often answer by calling their language by their own words. For example, Turkish is called "Turkçe" or the "Nihongo" is Japanese for the Japanese language. You may have to look up some languages or use a translation app. Essentially, inner speech is the language you use to talk to yourself.

Gannaway (1994) characterizes inner speech as "that reservoir of internalized thought and language on which we depend for communication". Typically, a bilingual or multilingual person can communicate well in more than one language. Some bilingual or multilingual speakers do not write in all their acquired languages. For example, some people only know environmental print or social language signs in their native or other languages. I call this low-literate, and not knowing any of one's written language is considered illiterate. Around the world including here in the United States there are countless adults who remain illiterate all their lives. Speaking a language does not guarantee the ability to read and write. Bilingual or multilingual speakers who do read and write in their native language have formed a better basis of their English literacy development.

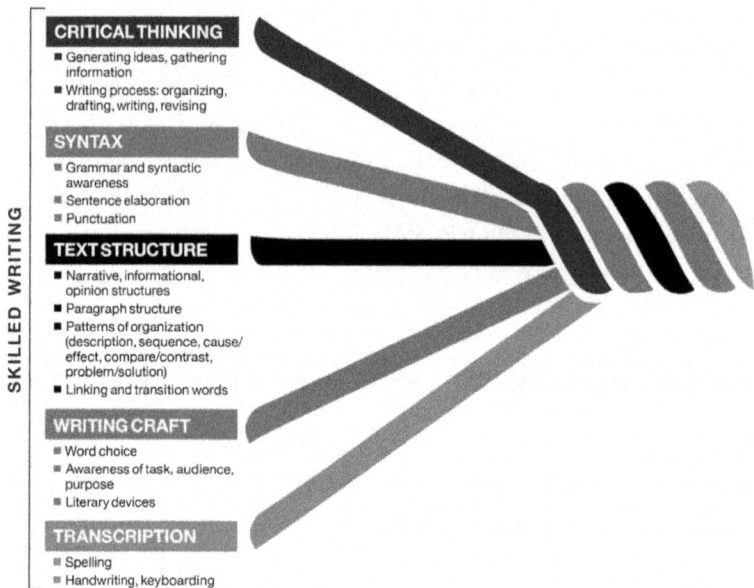

Figure 2.2 Sedita's Writing Rope

Teaching ELs writing becomes an integral part of advancing English acquisition and fluency. Figure 2.2 shows the complexities involved in writing in one's first language. Writers in any language must pull together their ideas and put them into established patterns of the language with effective word choice and proper spelling. That is a remarkable capability. Multilingual writers must also grapple with all these aspects of recording their thoughts in another language's pattern and norms. This may explain why writing is usually ELs' last developed skill set.

Seen as the culminating skill, writing provides an avenue for both learning and expressing learning. Before writing happens, however, ELs must integrate some English vocabulary and language systems through listening, speaking, and reading. The ability to write in a new language begins with the correlation between one's inner speech put into English words, phrases, and/or sentences. Authentic texts such as these student-created writing pieces provide real-world reading materials with more interest for

Newcomers than disconnected, unfamiliar readings within a commercial education program (Albiladi, 2019). However, both types of texts, authentic student generated and pre-designed, used in proper balance build literacy skills.

Reflection Questions:

1. How does structured literacy instruction differ for ELs and non-ELs?
2. Which aspect of literacy instruction is less critical for Newcomers to develop in the beginning stages of English literacy learning and why?
3. Writing is called the culminating skill, why is that and what challenges does that produce for Newcomers?

References

Albiladi, W. S. (2019). Exploring the use of written authentic materials in ESL reading classes: Benefits and challenges. *English Language Teaching, 12*(1). Published by Canadian Center of Science and Education.

Archer, A. L., & Hughes, C. A. (2011). *Explicit instruction: Effective and efficient teaching*. Guilford Press.

August, D., & Shanahan, T. (Eds.). (2006). *Developing literacy in second-language learners: Report of the national literacy panel on language-minority children and youth*. Routledge.

Gannaway, G. (1994). *Transforming mind: A critical cognitive activity*. Greenwood Publisher.

Krashen, S. D., & Terrell, T. D. (1983). *The natural approach: Language acquisition in the classroom*. Pergamon Press.

Moats, L. C. (2020). *Speech to print: Language essentials for teachers*. Brookes Publishing.

National Reading Panel (U.S.), & National Institute of Child Health and Human Development (U.S.). (2000). *Report of the national reading panel: Teaching children to read: An evidence-based assessment of the scientific research literature on reading and its implications for reading instruction*. U.S. Department of Health and Human Services/Public Health Service/National Institutes of Health/National Institute of Child Health and Human Development.

Scarborough, H. S. (2001). Connecting early language and literacy to later reading (dis)abilities: Evidence, theory, and practice. In S. Neuman & D. Dickinson (Eds.), *Handbook for research in early literacy* (pp. 97–110). Guilford Press.

Treiman, R. (2018). What research tells us about reading instruction. *Psychological Science in the Public Interest,19*(1), 1-4. https://doi.org/10.1177/1529100618772272

WIDA. (2020). *WIDA English language development standards framework, 2020 edition: Kindergarten–grade 12*. Board of Regents of the University of Wisconsin System.

Wolf-Greenberg, M., Horvath, T., & Krimmel, E. F. (2022). Three steps to create a designated eld curriculum aligned to academic content. *Journal of English Learner Education, 14*(1).

3 | **EL Writing Process for Newcomers**

The Writing Process versus EL Writing Process Protocol for Newcomers

In 1972, Donald M. Murray published his insightful article *Teach Writing as a Process, Not a Product,* which changed the landscape of writing instruction from focusing on the product to the process involved in writing (Murray, 1972). Murray believed that any writing task involved pre-writing, writing, and rewriting before producing a final version, and these steps required instruction, guidance, and practice.

In my own teaching and while observing fellow teachers, I realize that the usual way of teaching writing in classrooms these days often falls short for ELs, especially Newcomers, when it comes to learning academic English reading and writing skills. The pre-writing, writing or drafting, revising and editing, and publishing processes show effectiveness for native English speakers and higher-level ELs, but the systematic approach falls short for Newcomers who need targeted linguistic support.

The EL Writing Process is designed to fill in the gaps for Newcomers that the writing process does not address such as assumed letter sound correlation and English language patterns. Using EL writing techniques and activities will accelerate Newcomers' writing and literacy skills by encouraging their self-expression and personal connection to English sounds, letters, words, and phrases over time. Table 3.1 gives you a visual of how you can seamlessly incorporate EL techniques into your writing process planning, delivery, and instruction. As many ESL specialists will attest, what you do for your ELs often benefits all students. Those students

DOI: 10.4324/9781003610595-5

Table 3.1 Integration of EL Writing Process

The Writing Process Instruction	The EL Writing Process Integration
Pre-writing Introduce the writing topic & task, completing a graphic organizer. **Writing** Write a rough draft based on task and graphic organizer. **Revising and Editing** Self-editing of writing with peer or teacher feedback, revising content, and correcting errors. **Publishing** The teacher decides how to display the writing pieces and assesses development from finalized writing version.	**Pre-writing** While introducing topic & task, provide level 1-appropriate materials and enhance visualization by modeling a final version of the writing task. **Writing** Draw or find an image as a guide for writing a first draft. Use of the Word Line tool minimizes writer's block for Newcomers. **Editing and Revising** Teachable moments through personalized error correction when teacher underwriting and personalized literacy instruction and phonics flexing allows the bilingual brain to associate English sounds to letters. **Publishing** Rewrite corrected words for repetition and acquisition to accelerate internalization of words Newcomers want to communicate – Track triumphs and trials to inform strategic instruction planning and mini lesson delivery for learning English patterns.

who do not need targeted linguistic support can continue writing while you deliver more foundational literacy strategies.

By integrating EL-focused techniques into your writing workshop practice, you can differentiate instruction and supply manageable learning opportunities for Newcomers. Figure 3.1 displays the eight EL techniques you can incorporate into your writing instruction to get Newcomers writing early instead of giving them coloring pages or simply copying meaningless words.

Some Newcomer may not know the English alphabet until they step into your classroom. I contend in this book that by consistently using these eight techniques, you will accelerate your Newcomer's literacy development compared to Newcomers who are tasked with simply copying

EL WRITING PROCESS

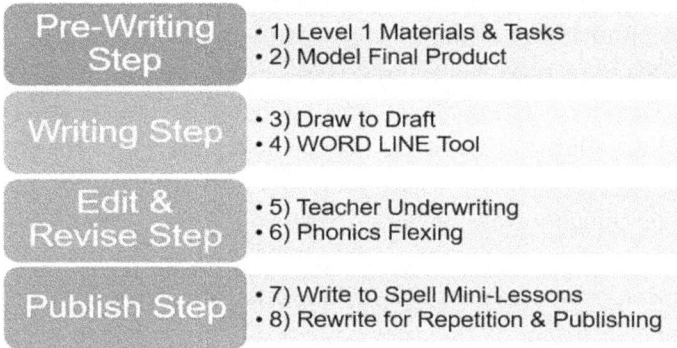

Pre-Writing Step	• 1) Level 1 Materials & Tasks • 2) Model Final Product
Writing Step	• 3) Draw to Draft • 4) WORD LINE Tool
Edit & Revise Step	• 5) Teacher Underwriting • 6) Phonics Flexing
Publish Step	• 7) Write to Spell Mini-Lessons • 8) Rewrite for Repetition & Publishing

Figure 3.1 The EL Writing Process and techniques
Source: Created by Eugenia Krimmel, 2025.

without comprehension of words they see on a word wall. You begin by building their understanding of the topic and English words surrounding that topic, but you also furnish your Newcomers with opportunities to write what they want to say. In turn those words they search for to communicate stay in their minds better.

Translanguaging When Writing in English

Create the need for Newcomers to write in English but allow them to first write in whatever language they wish. Some will mix English with first-language words which is a natural part of a Newcomer's language acquisition. This is known as the assets-based strategy *translanguaging*. They will translate back in their minds, so let that come out on paper. They will write native language labels on their drawings and graphic organizers during the draw-to-draft step. To the best of your ability and your Newcomer's, try to convert all words into English during the TU step. Allowing translanguaging during the writing process may prevent writer's block for Newcomers. Celebrate that they are writing in whichever language at first. They will write more in English as their proficiency increases with your encouragement or sometimes with your insistence.

45

PF is an equally critical EL technique integrated into the writing process for Newcomers. Not only does it allow for personalized phonics and spelling instruction, but this activity affords the bilingual brain time to process the same pattern of sounds several times per word. PF is a unique two-pronged strategy as both an error correction technique and personalized literacy instruction at the basic letter-sound level. The powerful punch of this combination aims to provide much-needed explicit English pattern teaching for Newcomers in grades 3–12. As Newcomers improve over the school year, they will need less PF on your part; however, as they encounter more and more new English words and phrases, they may need occasional PF again.

Rewriting for publishing Newcomers' writing cannot be overlooked as an important step in their writing development. The purpose for writing gives writers a goal to work on and purpose for their communication efforts. By rewriting after TU, Newcomers begin the process of internalizing patterns of English with the words *they* want to write thus making the activity more impactful and engaging. Plan mini lessons for targeted literacy instruction to reinforce phonics, spelling, and/or writing English patterns as Newcomers need to deepen their language acquisition.

Publishing their work for classmates and teachers to see brings the writing full circle from thought (in any language) to reality. They can see their own English capabilities on paper or screen. Lastly, after all the EL writing techniques were integrated into the writing workshop or project time, measure their writing with a single-point rubric or other assignment-specific measuring tool.

I also encourage you to track Newcomers' progress over the school year. Using the same assessment as before, do a few quick testing-segment sessions, when possible, over the course of a week to measure decoding, encoding, and written word stages of each Newcomer. You could do this at the beginning and end of each school quarter or simply when the Newcomer arrives and at the end of the year. Tracking progress lies at the heart of the EL Writing Process. Your instruction will be informed, strategic, and targeted as a result of stopping to note each Newcomer's triumphs and trials of learning academic English.

This book and the techniques described equip you in your literacy teaching practice with a how-to guide instead of just a checklist of what-to-do actions. Far too many books give you the why and what without the "how-to". As you read about each technique, you will be empowered with confidence in your capability to teach Newcomers literacy through a systematic, structured protocol from day one.

Getting Ready for EL Writing Process Integration

As with any instruction, you will need to do a few steps of preparation. To start, I suggest these simple steps:

1. Know as much about your ELs' home languages as possible. Why? The characteristics of their language may explain why they mispronounce certain sounds like "th" or mix sounds like "ch" with "sh". Teachers who do not know these language traits tend to refer to ELs for speech services when the ELs are simply transferring from their first language. To learn more, check out Appendix A: the Cross-Linguistic Contrast Chart or explore websites such as *omniglot.com* and *mylanguages.org*.
2. Learn the English proficiency level of your ELs to scaffold for each in appropriate measure. Newcomers and Level-1 ELs benefit most from all the EL techniques. As ELs advance, they may no longer need techniques like PF and draw-to-draft. That will be up to your professional discretion. Remember to grow with your ELs as they grow linguistically.
3. Identify which ELs are Newcomers and assess their English phonology, phonics, spelling, and basic writing skills if any. Use the Newcomer Literacy Survey in Chapter 4 of this book to gauge the targeted skills of foundational literacy. You can administer the survey sections in parts over a week or complete it in one sitting as Newcomers join your class.

    For a writing sample to complete the baseline survey, you could also assign a low-stakes, familiar topic quick writing prompt to get an idea of what each Newcomer can produce in English literacy if anything. Another possibility is to use Newcomers' first writing piece during EL writing as the baseline. In Chapter 8 spelling and EL writing scales are provided for you to gauge and monitor literacy progress at the very basic level before using other rubrics that assume the production of English sentences. See Chapter 4 for the Newcomer Literacy Survey tracking record, teacher instructions, and student booklet for writing. These resources are also found in the Supporting Materials folder as Newcomer Literacy Survey.

4. Speak to Newcomers a bit more slowly with repetition and gestures for better communication. Oral language plays a vital part in literacy; however, Newcomers are generally in their "silent period". That is a period of time when ELs' brains are taking in new, unfamiliar sounds and written language and then organizing them before they produce words. That mental process takes time and practice, so most simply cannot or do not produce the new language in the early stages (Krashen, 1981). Even though you are gearing up to have Newcomers do quick writes or writer's workshop time, use gestures, visuals, high-frequency words, and repetition as you speak giving them valuable exposure to English.

5. Know the rules! Refer to reputable phonics and spelling sources based on the Orton-Gillingham approach to literacy. I recommend watching videos or reading information from Reading Horizons (2015) although your school may prefer to use another phonics instructional program. The videos by Reading Horizons on YouTube give you a systematic technique for teaching and understanding English phonics and decoding skills that will help you help your Newcomers.

6. Find a good grammar resource, too. ELs will ask why we say things the way we do, and you should know why. This goes to credibility and respect; however, if you truly do not know, tell them you will get back to them on that linguistic point. I recommend bookmarking the English Grammar website https://www.englishgrammar.org/ as a reference when you need to understand a grammar point. There are rules and self-testing practice to upgrade your grammar game!

Reflection Questions:

1. Describe the similarities between the general education writing process and EL Writing Process. What are the differences between these two protocols?

2. Why should you, as a writing teacher of ELs, integrate EL-focused techniques for your Newcomers?

3. Describe translanguaging in your own words through your experience or what you learned in this chapter.

References

Krashen, S. (1981). *Second language acquisition and second language learning.* Pergamon Press.

Murray, D. (1972, Fall). *Teach writing as a process not product* (pp. 11–14). The Leaflet/New England Association of Teachers of English.

Reading Horizons. (2015, January 19). *Reading horizons method – method overview* [Video]. YouTube. https://youtu.be/lQp0VZtq41k?si=SaRkSPRWuBts-3-o

The Eight Techniques of the EL Writing Process

Pre-Writing Step	• 1) Level 1 Materials & Tasks • 2) Model Final Product
Writing Step	• 3) Draw to Draft • 4) WORD LINE Tool
Edit & Revise Step	• 5) Teacher Underwriting • 6) Phonics Flexing
Publish Step	• 7) Write to Spell Mini-Lessons • 8) Rewrite for Repetition & Publishing

DOI: 10.4324/9781003610595-6

4 Beginning Baseline for Tracking Progress

The EL Writing Process is a personalized approach to literacy instruction woven into your writing workshop practices. Research conducted by Cummins (1991) and Collier (1987) has consistently highlighted the importance of obtaining baseline measures of initial English literacy skills for Newcomers. According to their studies, baseline assessments provide you with valuable insights into each learner's current English proficiency level to address the specific needs of each student.

Studies done by August and Shanahan (2006) have demonstrated that understanding a student's baseline literacy skills allows you to identify areas of strength and weakness, enabling you to target effective phonics, spelling, and writing strategies for Newcomers to progress along the English literacy continuum. This targeted support has been shown to significantly enhance language acquisition and literacy development among ELs along their language learning journey.

As a result of their research, Genesee (1994) and Thomas and Collier (2002) emphasize the importance of baseline measures in monitoring students' progress over time. Regular assessment and monitoring, as suggested by their studies, help you evaluate the effectiveness of instructional strategies you use, leading to improved academic outcomes for all ELs. To that end, you should plan to get a baseline of foundational skills for each of your Newcomers shortly after arriving in your class. Knowing your Newcomers' writing skills informs you on how to differentiate your writing instruction by EL groups.

DOI: 10.4324/9781003610595-7

The Newcomer Literacy Survey

Which assessment tool should I use for literacy pre-assessment and progress monitoring throughout the school year? Keep in mind, unless an instrument is designed for second language learners, assessment instruments like Heggerty, CORE Phonics Screener, DIBELS, iReady, and Acadience, among others, are all normed to native English-speaking students. Therefore, Newcomer performance will typically lag behind their peers. Other than EL screeners used to measure English proficiency in all four language skills, you will be hard pressed to find a foundational literacy assessment designed for Newcomers.

For that reason, I studied the many native-English literacy assessments and the skills involved to design the Newcomer Literacy Survey found in Appendices B–D. The aspects of foundational literacy you will measure include the following:

Phonological Awareness
Phonics
Decoding
Encoding (Spelling)
Basic Sentence/Question Formation

The Newcomer Literacy Survey & Tracking Record was designed for you to record and measure various aspects of English literacy while noting the triumphs and trials for each Newcomer. Triumphs are those linguistic points a Newcomer produces, indicating the point is internalized to the working memory if not the long-term memory. On the other hand, trials are those items not yet acquired because Newcomers either do not produce them or produce them incorrectly. Record these results to share with Newcomers, their families, administrators, and fellow teachers. The Tracking Record in Appendix B is followed by Teacher Administration Instructions in Appendix C, and the Student Booklet in Appendix D can be printed out for use as needed. All of these documents are available in the Support Materials.

Measuring Phonological Knowledge of Newcomers

The first step to learning any language is to acquire its individual sounds. Newcomers must learn to decipher and recognize phonemes within spoken words to be able to decode and write these new English sound combinations. Those sound combinations eventually lead to comprehension. If Newcomers spell words incorrectly when attempting to write even in the very early days, it could be because they do not distinguish the sound in a word or have not yet internalized that sound-letter correspondence. To that end, keep ongoing records of Newcomer's ability to hear all the phonemes of English using phonological assessments and tracking records so you are better informed to plan effective literacy instruction.

Phonics and Decoding Knowledge Inventory

Naming letters is an important component to reading and writing development, therefore, measuring the number of known letter names should be tracked for Newcomers while keeping in mind which phonemes they have or do not have in their first language. You may easily have Newcomers who speak a wide variety of languages you know little about and that is perfectly normal. For example, knowing that a Turk will produce /j/ sound for the English letter "c" explains that error in early attempts to write the /j/ sound in English. When that Turkish-speaking Newcomer writes a "j" for the /j/ sound, you will know they internalized that sound-letter correspondence. You will find that when comparing Newcomers' errors to what you learn about their languages, most, not all, errors will make sense. Appendix A serves as a starting point for you by contrasting several languages of Newcomers in our U.S. schools today.

EL Spelling Levels

Beyond letters and sounds, being able to spell words in English is an incredible accomplishment with all rules and exceptions. Think about it. English pulled words and spelling rules from a variety of sources: Greek, Latin, and Celtic languages like Dutch, just to name a few. As the English-speaking world interacted with other world cultures, spelling took on even more new patterns. And now in our modern world of business and text messaging, conventional spelling rules cause even more confusion. They may see a "nite mart" sign instead of "night market" or "Kwik Serv" for "quick service". Text messaging in English led many of my high school Newcomers to write words "cuz" for "because" and "laf" for "laugh" as if the texting forms were correct spelling forms.

Fluent spelling is an important part of fluent writing. For your Newcomers, however, correct spelling takes up a good part of their cognitive resources to organize and express their ideas in English (Lenski & Verbruggen, 2010). What you will notice over time will confirm research that shows increased spelling automaticity builds Newcomers' English communication confidence and fluency. To know if your Newcomers' spelling improved, you should have a means to collect this data point for each of your Newcomers' triumphs and trials both during TU and targeted spelling assessments such as a spelling inventory.

Unlike native English-speaking students, Newcomers have a similar progression along the continuum of spelling stages for reasons more closely related to their first language (L1) influence rather than their cognitive age. Hence, older Newcomers feel "stupid" and avoid writing because they think they should progress through the continuum more quickly than children learning their L1.

EL Spelling Stages align with those developed by researcher Ronald Cramer (1983) whose spelling development continuum flows from the *Words Their Way Framework*: Pre-phonetic stage, Phonetic Stage, Patterns Within Words Stage, Syllable Juncture Stage, and Meaning Derivation Stage of good spelling (Bear et al., 2019). Hamdan and Al-Zahrani (2020) uses Cramer's spelling stages to measure written work of Arabic-speaking middle-school students who study English as a New Language (ENL). Table 4.1 outlines EL spelling development progression for you to map over time.

Table 4.1 EL Spelling Development Progression Scale

Stage 1	Stage 2	Stage 3	Stage 4	Stage 5
Pre-phonetic stage	**Phonetic Stage**	**Patterns Within Words Stage**	**Syllable Juncture Stage**	**Meaning Derivation Stage**
• ELs may scribble or make marks not resembling English letters • Simply copy letters. Little concept of English sound-letter correlation. • Unfamiliar with the Latin script.	• Increased letter-sound correlations in their writing but not complete spelling. • Consonants are more often represented than vowels (long or short) • First language (L1) interferes in proper letter use.	• Writing shows EL knows not a 1-sound, 1-letter system in English • More often writing correct patterns of blends, digraphs, and long vowel teams • Increasing, but still inconsistent, correct spelling	• Errors occur more often where syllables meet in words when double letters, change in letter, or omitted letters occur • Overgeneralized spelling rules occur less frequently yet still contribute to errors • Internalized more English spelling patterns	• Shows a spelling-meaning relationship in both decoding and encoding • Fewer spelling errors • More correct spelling when taking notes or dictation showing advanced level of spelling based on semantics

Adapted from Cramer, R. (1998). *The spelling connection: Integrating reading, writing, and spelling instruction.* Guilford Press and Hamdan, M. H., & Al-Zahrani, M. A. S. (2020). Development of English spelling acquisition stages of Saudi intermediate school students. *Arab World English Journal, 11*(2), 232–242. https://dx.doi.org/10.24093/awej/vol11no2.16

The EL-Spelling Inventory assessment is recommended to use for Newcomers because it connects non-verbal and verbal cues with Newcomers so they can associate a spoken word with a mental image when given lists of words to spell.

Give this same list of words with images to your Newcomers multiple times within a school term or quarter to chart encoding progress. As spelling improves, change out words and images with new and reviewed spelling patterns. Be sure to vary the syllables, morphology, and spelling

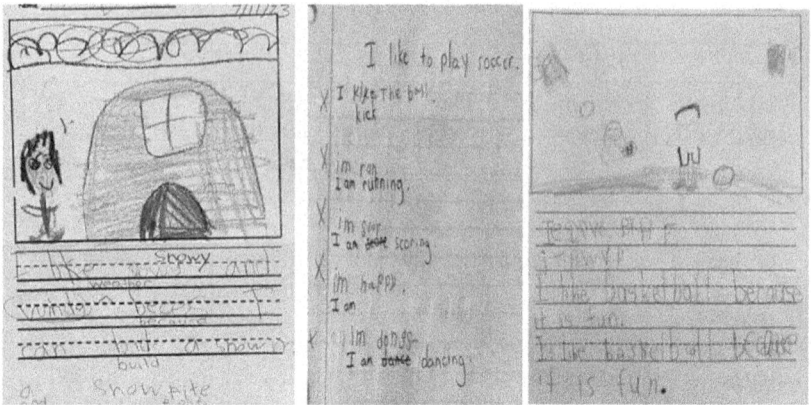

Figure 4.1 Examples of Newcomer writing

Source: Photo of Newcomer student writing samples by Eugenia Krimmel during Millersville University's ESL Clinical Practicum, 2022 and 2023.

points to effectively assess the literacy attempts of your Newcomers. I also encourage you to change out the words and images in the spelling inventory after you use them three times. Plan the aspects of spelling you want to measure when choosing new spelling words in the inventory. Record the results in the Newcomer Literacy Tracking Record.

What Does Newcomer Writing Mean?

Newcomer EL writing can be anything from scribbles attempting English letters to writing letters and words to short sentences, as shown in Figure 4.1.

Tracking Newcomers' Literacy Progress – Post-Assessments

After performing the TU and PF steps, record the triumphs and trials you see in each Newcomer's writing based on their first draft writing. This is your raw data from their first attempt which tells you a great deal about what they have in their heads. For example, many Newcomers drop the "n" in "nd" words like "friend or find" because they have not internalized that ending blend in English. That combination of sounds may not exist in their first language much like "mj" doesn't exist in English, yet it does in other languages. Another issue that may appear in Newcomer early writing is incorrect vowel sounds such as writing an "i" for the long /e/ sound as in "ich" for "each" and "grin" for "green".

During phonics flexing, you will consciousness-raise these errors to draw their minds' attention to these English features. In addition, you want to keep records of those errors to address them in mini lessons or individual writer's checklists. The EL writer's checklist serves as a writing guide that can be expanded to include other elements. Review and show all the points so Newcomers have some idea of your expectations for writing in academic English.

During either the rewriting or publishing step in your writing workshop cycle, you want to conduct a quick post-assessment similar to your pre-assessment. You will track the same skills you measured in the pre-assessment; phonological deciphering skills, to know if an EL hears and distinguishes one sound or group of words from others. Phonics skill measures center on a Newcomer's sound-letter connections.

Spelling skills from pre-test to post-test measure beyond phonics to learned patterns of English which will impact their writing fluency over time.

Lastly, review their writing pieces and record their triumphs and trials on a sentence level.

Writing Skills Assessments: Tracking Triumphs and Trials

As Newcomers relate their real or imaginary stories during EL Writing Process workshop sessions, you should keep records of their sentence-level communicative English forms and functions when possible. For recording accuracy, I recommend you use the ELPA21 Writing Rubrics Grades 2–3 (ELPA21, n.d.) for Newcomers of all ages because these excellent holistic rubrics are basic enough to capture their written abilities at this linguistic stage yet robust measurements for all levels. I find the ELPA21 rubrics by writing genre to truly make sense for the various types of writing tasks we teach throughout the school year such as picture captions and short storyboard writing. Personally, I find WIDA's writing rubrics to be far too generic and more difficult to measure Newcomer's basic writing.

Reflection Questions:

1. How can understanding a Newcomer's phonological awareness and spelling development help you differentiate writing instruction in your classroom?
2. What challenges might arise when using literacy assessments designed for native English speakers with Newcomers, and how can the Newcomer Literacy Survey address these gaps?
3. In what ways can tracking Newcomers' literacy triumphs and trials over time enhance their confidence and motivation in learning to write in English?

References

August, D., & Shanahan, T. (Eds.). (2006). *Developing literacy in second-language learners: Report of the national literacy panel on language-minority children and youth*. Routledge.

Bear, D., Invernizzi, M., Templeton, S., & Johnston, F. (2019). *Words their way: Word study for phonics, vocabulary, and spelling instruction* (7th ed.). Pearson Education.

Collier, V. P. (1987). Age and rate of acquisition of second language for academic purposes. *TESOL Quarterly, 21*, 617–641.

Cramer, R. L. (1983). *Spelling for teachers*. Addison-Wesley.

Cummins, J. (1991). Interdependence of first- and second-language proficiency in bilingual children. In E. Bialystok (Ed.), *Language processing in bilingual children* (pp. 70–89). Cambridge University Press.

ELPA21 Writing Rubrics Grades 2–3. (n.d.). *Elpa21 writing rubrics grade 2–3*. https://www.ode.state.or.us/wma/teachlearn/testing/resources/elpa21_writing_rubrics_g2-3.pdf

Genesee, F. (Ed.). (1994). *Educating second language children: The whole child, the whole curriculum, the whole community*. Cambridge University Press.

Hamdan, H., & Al-Zahrani, M. A. S. (2020). Development of English spelling acquisition stages of Saudi intermediate school students. *Arab World English Journal, 11*(2). https://doi.org/10.2139/ssrn.3649315

Lenski, S., & Verbruggen, F. (2010). *Writing instruction and assessment for English language learners K-8* (Vol. 12, pp. 126–127, 147–148). Guilford Press.

Thomas, W. P., & Collier, V. P. (2002). *A national study of school effectiveness for language minority students' long-term academic achievement.* Center for Research on Education, Diversity & Excellence (CREDE).

5 The Pre-Writing Step

Overview of the Pre-Writing Step

The pre-writing stage is an essential step in the writing process, and it involves activities that writers undertake before putting pen to paper or fingers to keyboard. While different researchers may use slightly different terminology or frameworks, there are some common elements emphasized by top researchers in the field of writing studies. One of the key components of pre-writing is brainstorming. Scholars such as Elbow (1998) and Murray (1972) emphasized the importance of freewriting to explore ideas about a topic and overcome writer's block. By allowing for uninhibited expression and capturing spontaneous thoughts, writers can uncover valuable insights and connections that contribute to the development of their writing piece. Elbow and Murray's ascertains the language experience approach (LEA) used as a language acquisition strategy to accelerate internalization of words and phrases.

The concept of pre-writing is also closely linked to the planning and outlining stages. Scholars like Wilber and Sullivan (2016) advocate for the creation of outlines as a roadmap for the writing process. Outlining helps writers organize their thoughts coherently, ensuring a logical flow of ideas within the composition. It acts as a guide for drafting and minimizes the risk of writer's block. Because writing is not a single-step process, preparing to write by brainstorming ideas, learning new words, and outlining one's thoughts set writers up for a more organized, cohesive, and interesting final writing piece. Newcomers benefit from a well-planned, modified, and timely pre-writing session to start with confidence.

DOI: 10.4324/9781003610595-8

EL WRITING PROCESS

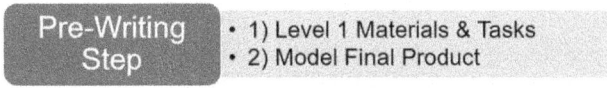

Pre-Writing Step	• 1) Level 1 Materials & Tasks • 2) Model Final Product

Image 5.1 The pre-writing step

EL Techniques to Integrate into Your Pre-Writing Practice

Many teachers I have trained in the EL Writing Process tell me they thought they introduced a topic and task for their writing workshop sessions effectively until they learned how much all Newcomers needed to:

- Recall or build background knowledge
- Know English vocabulary words to write
- Spell the English words they want to say
- "Say it in English" in the right word order patterns
- Know how to fill and use graphic organizers which some Newcomers have never seen before

Getting Started – Introducing the Writing Task and Topic

Pre-writing steps begin with any one of several introduction strategies such as watching a video clip, reading mentor texts aloud, discussing a topic-related question, showing an image, or asking a question of the whole class. Use a wide variety of fun introduction strategies and activities to begin a new writing workshop. These strategies benefit ELs and non-ELs as you incorporate ways to build or recall knowledge of the topic using gestures, good images, and/or keywords. You can also use Newcomers' first language if available but add the English equivalent as soon as possible to begin the connection-to-acquisition process. Connections can also be made through LPA activities.

The Language Experience Approach in EL Writing Instruction

For learners entering the new or additional language acquisition stage of English literacy, LPA activities prove to be effective. The LPA employs ELs' life experiences with their linguistic funds of knowledge while developing their English skills and proficiency. This approach draws on the experiences of a learner as content material for instructional purposes. Nessel and Dixon state that "in all forms of LEA, the central principle is to use the student's own vocabulary, language patterns, and background of experiences to create reading texts, making reading [and writing] a significant and enjoyable process" (2008, p. 1).

Application of LEA pedagogy includes the use of reading and writing techniques that progressively develop ELs' skills from dependent to independent learners leading to fuller access to the curriculum and more fluent communication skills. At the beginning stages of language acquisition, listening comprehension or the ability to distinguish one sound from another or one word within a spoken sentence is a critical step prior to literacy skill development; however, time rarely allows a K 12 or an adult student to develop their "English ear" before tackling written assignments. While *reading* encompasses both decoding and comprehension, *writing* includes both spelling and meaningful communication.

Like all learners, Newcomers of all ages need to develop all these skills in an authentic way for true acquisition. LEA-type classroom activities should be included routinely for ELs of all ages to incorporate oral and written English. Literacy skills involve not only decoding and encoding but also comprehension. The LEA activities shown in Table 5.1 may be familiar to you, but I challenge you to see each in a different light for language acquisition goals:

In addition, Newcomers require modified materials and tasks in the pre-writing step to improve accessibility to the topic and assignment of the writing workshop. Without Level 1-appropriate add-ins, Newcomers struggle to comprehend the information and express themselves. Teachers and Newcomers can easily fall back into a familiar routine of having them only coloring and copying for writing. You can make a difference and accelerate their literacy skills by getting your Newcomers to write right away!

Table 5.1 Language Experience Approach Activity Ideas

Interactive reading and large-chart literacy sessions for sharing ideas	Wordless book writing in pairs or small groups to tell the story	Shared experiences such as field trips or virtual fields trips – recalling details
Write about in-class science, math, or social studies discoveries	Literature circles and shared book reading to recount and analyze information	One-to-one tutoring sessions labeling an image or writing short description using student's own words

A Word About Copying

Essentially the difference between copying with or without compre-hension is a matter of internal versus external motivation. Copying with comprehension occurs as Newcomers see words on the wall or in text and choose to express their own thoughts with the selected words in semi-controlled or free-write activities. It is what they wanted to say in writing. Copying without comprehension is routinely having Newcomers write from word walls in controlled activities like sentence completion from a word bank. This type of task has its place in language development instruction, but during writing workshops, the freedom to write one's own thoughts connects to Newcomers' internal desire to be understood. In turn, this adds to the bilingual brain's ability to attend to certain words in working memory and move it along to long-term memory.

Technique #1 – Level 1 Materials and Tasks

Several graduate student teacher trainees in my ESL Clinical Practicum program who modeled and provided simplified graphic organizers as part of the pre-writing step found that Newcomers more easily trans-ferred their thoughts off their simplified graphic organizer to their writing and significantly lessened writer's block compared to their first attempts at writing without a Level 1-appropriate organizer. Other teacher train-ees in the practicum noted that model texts were too difficult for their Newcomers, so they found lower Lexile-leveled texts on the same topic.

All the teachers found that co-constructing word walls for the writing task improved Newcomers' writing fluency. These examples of Level 1 materials may seem obvious in some ways but take nothing for granted. You have to present as basic materials as you can find for Newcomers and then add back more text, graphics, and visuals as possible over the school year.

What Are Level 1 Materials?

As you now know, Level 1 in the world of SLA is the first stage of acquiring a new language. ELs at this stage are at the letter-to-word level of taking in English both orally and through literacy. However, each EL is fluent in their native language; therefore, they can cognitively think complex thoughts just like their peers. English, of course, brings up linguistic roadblocks to expressing those thoughts for a year or more within the five to seven years ELs require to reach near-peer proficiency (Cummins, 1979; Collier & Thomas, 1993).

As their teacher of writing in this initial stage, purposefully modified materials allow Newcomers to overcome, even partially, the language barrier. Provide simplified graphic organizers, reduced text, and pre-teach or reteach lesson vocabulary using good visuals. Avoid the trap many educators fall into when thinking of Newcomers as less intelligent, delayed in thought, and dare I say "dumb" as many have said to me over the years. No EL deserves to have a deficit-based mindset in their teacher. You should always ask yourself the assets-based question, "How can I get them [your Newcomers and all ELs] to . . .?"

Examples:

How can I get them to write a sentence with adjectives and adverbs?
How can I get them to use gerunds properly?
How can I get them to write a good paragraph?
How can I get them to use context clues to understand text better?

Your responsibility is to scaffold up to meet their language needs and then pull back the support as they acquire more and more English proficiency. Your mindset is assets-based and respectful of their genius behind the language barrier. With that in mind, you will find integrating Level 1 materials and tasks into your pre-writing practices effective and seamless.

EL Writing Integration

As you deliver your opening strategies, think of ways to scaffold up with linguistic, visual, and graphic support. While many people think translated versions of texts are an end-all-be-all, the simple fact is not all Newcomers or Level 1 ELs are literate or they may be low literate in their first language for a variety of reasons – very young, inadequate literacy instruction, learning differences, or possibly did not attend school previously. Know your Newcomers by figuring out if they are literate in their first language. Ask them to write their name and a description of their favorite place or person. If they can do that with ease, they are literate. If they struggle or refuse, they are most likely unable to read and write in their first language and that information will give you great insight into their English language starting point.

Other linguistic supports beyond translation, visuals, and graphic supports, including labeled images or objects, synonyms or antonyms, and categorized word walls for word associations, are shown in Table 5.2.

Language Strategies: Reduced Text

You may choose to introduce a writing workshop topic through reading materials such as articles or stories. Because your Newcomers may understand less of the text than other students, consider providing them with reduced text versions so they grapple with fewer words in the same

Table 5.2 Scaffolding Up Strategies for the Pre-Writing Step

Language	Visual	Graphic
- Reduced text - Synonyms = - Antonyms ≠	- Realia - Good versus Bad visuals - Labeled images	- Simplified organizers - Infographics

amount of time. Some book series have reduced text versions for struggling readers and/ELs, but many do not.

How can you reduce text without rewriting an article or story yourself? One way is to give Newcomers only part of the text at a time. The "chunking reading trick" is like taking a big puzzle and breaking it into smaller, easier pieces. Giving Newcomers pieces of text at a time helps them figure out important words to get the gist of the passage before getting another key portion of the text. OR give them only the beginning and have them interact in literature circles or other cooperative learning activities to learn more.

Digital versions of text are more easily reduced through AI tools such as MagicSchool, ChatGPT, Copilot, Khanmigo, and Brisk Teaching, among others. I used AI to help me turn a typical high school English Language Arts lesson text on analyzing two literary pieces through compare and contrast into a Level 1 mentor text. The original mentor text provided was made by me but could be teacher-made or even a result of an interactive class activity put into writing. The second text is a version of the same mentor text reduced through MagicSchool's Text Leveler tool. Higher-proficiency ELs and non-ELs are given the original version while Newcomers are given the reduced version allowing them time to figure out cognates, translate words if possible, or look for familiar words on labeled images, word walls, or in graphic organizers for enhanced understanding.

Original Example Text

Literary works provide readers with powerful stories that explore various aspects of life, society, and human nature. The two well-known novels "The Grapes of Wrath" and "To Kill a Mockingbird" delve into different time periods and settings while addressing similar themes. In this assignment, we explore the similarities and differences between these two exceptional literary works in terms of theme and setting.

Theme

Both "The Grapes of Wrath" and "To Kill a Mockingbird" tackle significant societal themes that resonate with readers of all ages.

A. In "The Grapes of Wrath", written by John Steinbeck, the theme of social injustice takes center stage. The novel portrays the harsh realities faced by farmers during the Great Depression, highlighting the struggles of the Joad family as they are displaced from their Oklahoma farm and journey to California in search of a better life. Steinbeck's work examines the exploitation of the working class and the unequal distribution of wealth during that time, emphasizing the importance of unity and collective action.

B. On the other hand, Harper Lee's "To Kill a Mockingbird" explores the theme of racial inequality and prejudice in the 1930s American South. Through the eyes of Scout Finch, the novel sheds light on the injustice faced by African Americans and the impact it has on individuals and communities. Lee's work challenges societal norms and encourages empathy and understanding, urging readers to confront racism and promote equality.

Settings

The settings of both novels play a crucial role in shaping the narratives and conveying the social and historical context of their respective time periods.

A. "The Grapes of Wrath" is primarily set during the Great Depression and takes readers on a journey across the United States. Beginning in Oklahoma's Dust Bowl region, the Joad family travels westward to California, the land of promise and opportunity. This setting allows Steinbeck to explore the vast economic disparities and expose the exploitation and difficulties faced by migrant workers.

B. "To Kill a Mockingbird" is set in the fictional town of Maycomb, Alabama, during the 1930s. This Southern setting provides a backdrop for the deeply ingrained racism and prejudice that exist within the community. The town's closely knit society and its accompanying social dynamics shape the experiences and challenges faced by Scout and the other characters in the novel.

In summary, "The Grapes of Wrath" and "To Kill a Mockingbird" share common themes of social injustice and offer insightful characterizations. While "The Grapes of Wrath" focuses on the struggles of farmers during the Great Depression, "To Kill a Mockingbird" explores racial inequality in the American South. Both novels utilize their respective settings to highlight the social and historical contexts of their narratives. Through these works, readers gain valuable insights into different time periods and the enduring themes that continue to resonate with audiences today.

- Generated and edited from MagicSchool's Informational Text tool

Reduced Text: Level 1 version; add images where possible

I. Introduction

Let's talk about two special books!
    "The Grapes of Wrath" and "To Kill a Mockingbird".

II. Theme

A. "The Grapes of Wrath"
    1. Long ago, during a tough time called the Great Depression
    2. A family, the Joads, had a hard life
    3. The book talks about how some people were not treated fairly because they didn't have much money.
B. "To Kill a Mockingbird"
    1. A long time ago, in the southern part of the United States
    2. A young girl named Scout tells the story
    3. The book is about how some people were not treated well because of their skin color.

III. Settings

A. "The Grapes of Wrath"
    1. Long ago, in different parts of the United States
    2. During a time when many people didn't have enough money
    3. The book shows us how some poor people had a hard time with no money
B. "To Kill a Mockingbird"
    1. In a fake (not real) town called Maycomb

2. The book helps us understand how some people were not treated nicely because of how they looked.

- Generated and edited from MagicSchool's Informational Text tool

By reducing the "language load", meaning the number of words Newcomers' bilingual brains have to process, they can focus on the high-frequency and text-specific words to at least surmise the gist of the text. By bolding keywords and phrases, Newcomers will attend to those words first before they get mentally fatigued by figuring out what the text means. However, BOLDING does not equal or lead to comprehension. Bolded text simply grabs the bilingual brain's attention before trying to grapple with other words. Also, note how the reduced version included more familiar words than the original version. That can be done effortlessly within AI settings as you learn to use these valuable tools to help you save time and energy. Try AI tools to help you help your Newcomers.

Language Strategies: Synonyms and Antonyms for Vocabulary Teaching

By associating words in English, you build a Newcomer's vocabulary repertoire more quickly. *Synonym strands* are easy and quick to write on the board, on an index card, or on chart paper for the whole class to review. As said by many educators, "What you do for ELs, you benefit other students, too". This is one of those strategies to help all, so take 30 seconds to present synonym strands of three to five keywords from high-frequency words to academic or lesson-specific words when possible.

Table 5.3 illustrates synonym strands and Table 5.4 shows antonym rows as examples of how you can think through this Level 1 pre-writing technique. The equal sign shows similar significance even though there are differences in connotation or specific meanings, but at this stage, Newcomers need the overall meaning of the words. The unequal sign which you may have to demonstrate the meaning to Newcomers at first will indicate the opposite meaning.

Table 5.3 Synonym Strands Example

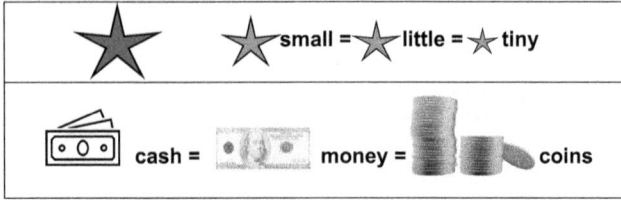

Table 5.4 Antonym Rows Example

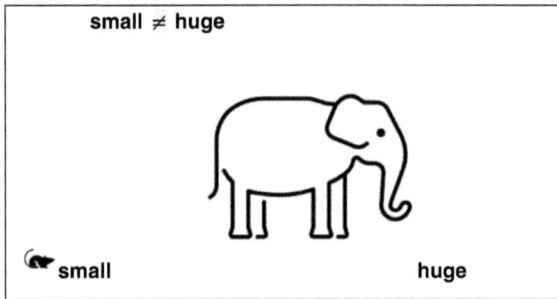

Educational neuroscience consultant David Sousa claims that for decades researchers have stated that our brains build on the familiar to learn more (2010). With that premise, effective vocabulary teaching moves from the familiar to the new related information. Newcomers know too little English, so how can this activity work? Use photos or gestures for common, high-frequency words whenever possible to give mental imagery. From this point, words are associated as similar or opposite.

Visual Strategies: Realia

Real objects or representations of real objects are called "realia" in the language-learning world. These are not images, but things you can touch, hold, or show in 3D to connect classroom learning to real life. Your use of multisensory realia in the pre-writing step benefits Newcomers who will connect new words to the objects through their five senses. Try to bring in objects from home or the classroom whenever possible, so that Newcomers can learn vocabulary for writing.

Visual Strategies: Good versus Bad Images

Because pictures and images are relied upon for comprehension by all readers, especially Newcomers, you want to be sure they are effective at communicating the right words. You want them to be good images for conceptual comprehension. Good images are straightforward, simple, and often labeled with the corresponding word. Bad images, as shown in Table 5.5, are indirect, generic, and can easily be meaningless or confusing. Some teachers believe if a word appears on a wall or handout, it will be understood. Simply posting the word as an image is useless for Newcomers. Those hold no value or meaning at all.

Abstract words are difficult to illustrate. The example above shows that "democracy" is often depicted as an American flag. A Newcomer looks at that image as a flag and still has no idea of what democracy is. Again, simply writing the word somewhere does not guarantee understanding any more than highlighting, bolding, or reading words aloud. These formatting techniques merely draw attention to the words which are a start, but good, effective images truly lead to better understanding. Choose images wisely and ask yourself if the student can get a proper mental image of the contextual word from that image.

Setting Up Word/Phrase Walls in Class or Digitally

The use of word walls and language phrase walls in writing is not new; however, for Newcomers these visual supports are crucial. Teachers set up a routine of how, where, and when to find word/phrase walls in the class. During the pre-writing step, add the walls or digital collections with accompanying images where possible. Review each word or phrase for enhanced comprehension. Bilingual picture dictionaries in paper or digital form also add to Newcomers' ability to write their thoughts down in English with more flow and fluency. Digital platforms like AutoDraw.com

Table 5.5 Good versus Bad Images

Good	Bad
Pet – **This image is good because a Newcomer will see an animal in a home with a happy family and will understand the relationship of the word "pet" to the concept of human-animal co-habiting in the image.**	**Pet –** **This image is bad because a Newcomer will see only a "dog", not a pet if you simply give a single animal or even a group of animals without showing the human-animal or pet connection.**
Democracy – This image is good because democracy is an abstract concept in many ways; however, this image is closer to its meaning than an American flag.	**Democracy –** This image is bad because a Newcomer sees the flag and may even think the word "democracy" is a flag in English.

or Bing Image Creator AI tool can help you design your own images to use in class.

Graphic Strategies: Infographics

An infographic is a visual representation of information, data, or knowledge, designed to present complex concepts or data in a clear, concise, and easily understandable format. Newcomers derive meaning from the combination of images, charts, and minimal text because infographics aim to communicate information quickly and effectively, making it more accessible and engaging for the audience. Present your topic and new vocabulary using infographics sometimes and see how well your Newcomers grasp both concepts and language. An infographic provides reasons to recycle through visual elements and language; however, the example shown in Figure 5.1 is an ineffective infographic because it is too busy with too many visuals. Although it is reduced compared to a long paragraph, it still has too many words on it.

Like good or bad images, you must choose good infographics, too. Are some simply writing labels with little informational value? Does the infographic have too much imagery that can be confusing? Does the infographic really enhance instruction for Newcomers? Figure 5.2 shows a better choice of infographic because it has labels with simple understandable images.

The advantages of infographics for Newcomers are obvious, but the choice of infographics in the pre-writing step can make or break their understanding of the concepts and related wording if not chosen or created carefully.

Graphic Strategies: Simplified Organizers

Graphic organizers are particularly beneficial for Newcomer ELs in K-12 writing instruction due to their ability to simplify complex language concepts in visual and/or graphic form and foster comprehension. For students who may be grappling with a new language, these visual tools serve as a bridge between their ideas and effective communication. Graphic organizers provide a tangible structure that helps ELs organize their thoughts,

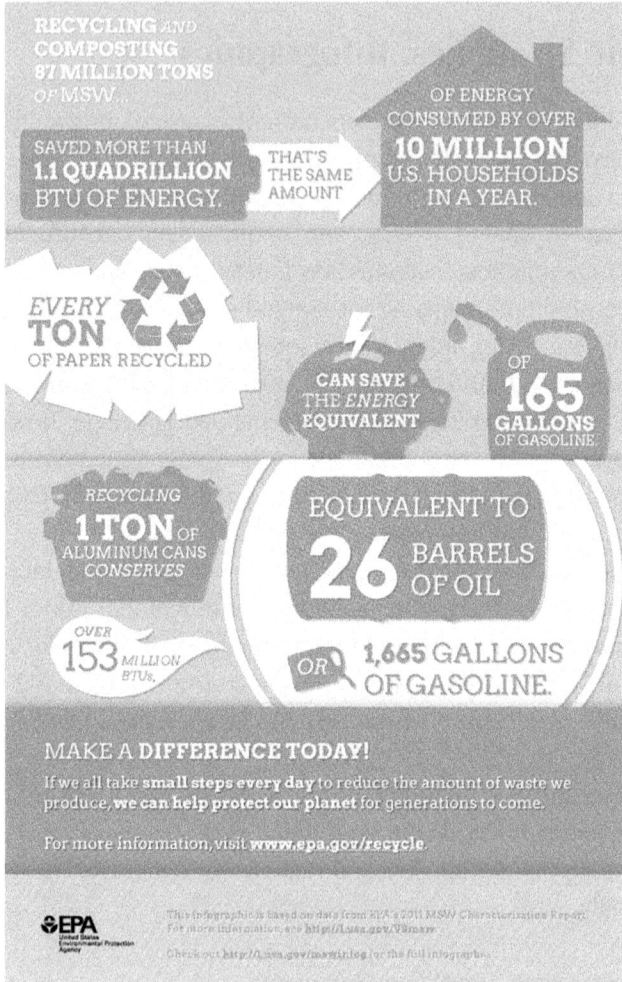

Figure 5.1 Example of an ineffective infographic for Newcomers

Source: USEPA Environmental Protection-Agency, Public domain, via Wikimedia Commons.

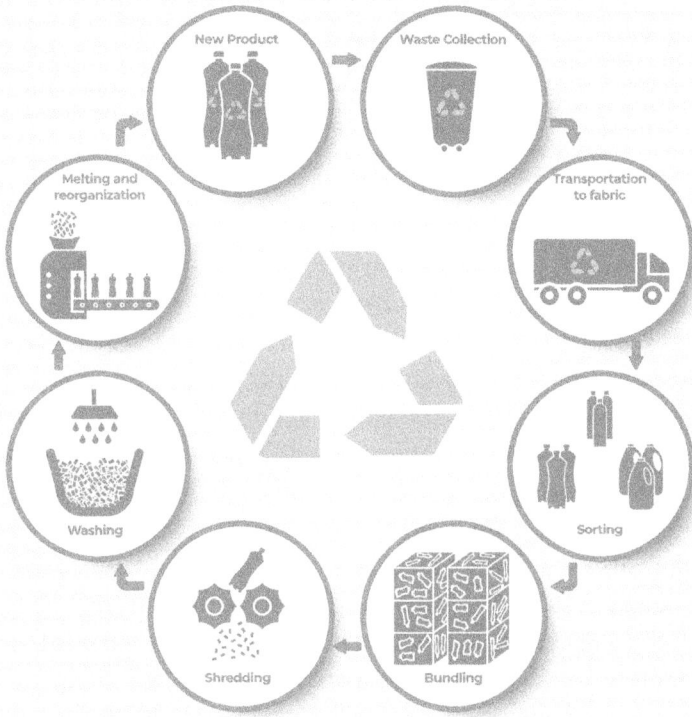

Figure 5.2 Example of a more effective infographic for Newcomers

aiding in simplified means of expressing their learning at the beginner level as they acquire more academic English. The visual representation of information also supports the understanding of English language conventions and sentence structures.

Additionally, graphic organizers offer a non-verbal means of representation of concepts and ways to express learning, allowing Newcomer students to convey their ideas with greater ease and confidence. Table 5.6 demonstrates the two-part T-chart that effectively shows the same or different relationships in a nonverbal way yet provides space to categorize vocabulary. This visual support enhances their language development and comprehension skills, enabling a smoother transition into ELP while simultaneously building a foundation for successful writing in academic contexts. As they

Table 5.6 Two-Part T-Chart Graphic Organizer for Newcomers

Natural Polymers	Human-made Polymers
Rubber	Teflon

World War II Allies	World War II Axis Powers
England France Russia America	Germany Italy Japan

gain more English proficiency, you will gradually increase the segments and complexity of graphic organizers for Newcomers.

An example of an effective, versatile Level 1-appropriate three-part graphic organizer for Newcomers is simply three boxes. These boxes can be used for narrative story elements, three steps in a process, three reasons for one's opinion, or three details supporting a topic sentence, among other uses. Figure 5.3 shows a three-part graphic organizer that was designed and shown to Newcomers by ESL teacher trainees during their clinical practicum. The teachers discovered the Newcomers were unable to complete longer graphic organizers during the pre-writing step. This graphic organizer was modeled by the ESL teacher trainees based on the writing task prompt, "What is a goal you achieved?" Note how one teacher trainee modeled this task with drawing first. It was later labeled and then Newcomers wrote simple sentences using the word wall terms and their own ideas by translating if they could.

When all the EL-writing teacher trainees simplified graphic organizers to two-part or three-part graphic organizers, their Newcomers found the tasks manageable to organize their thoughts and write simple sentences. After using three-part organizers in a few EL-writing workshops, Newcomers were able to build up to four-part segments for definitions, topic, and three details, a four-step process, or an argument claim, reasons, counterclaim, and rebuttal albeit in basic words and phrases. Newcomers, remember, are cognitively able to think critically but are behind the language barrier more than other ELs. Simplifying their materials and showing them models of how that can look at their level is key to getting them started with writing to learn.

Figure 5.4 shows a next level (four-part) graphic organizer for Newcomers. In this instance, EL-writing teacher trainees created and modeled

Figure 5.3 A three-part graphic organizer to show steps

Source: Photo of teacher-made Level 1 material by Eugenia Krimmel during Millersville University's ESL Clinical Practicum, 2023.

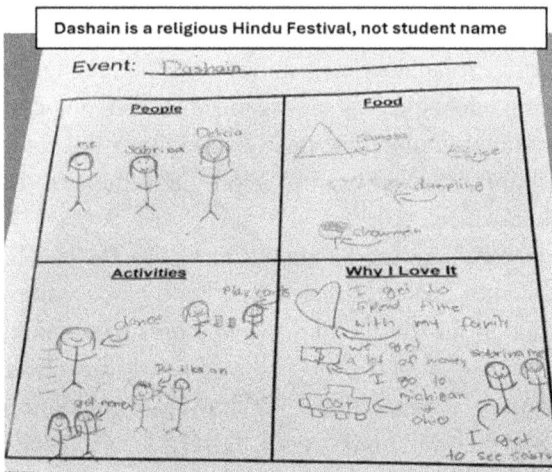

Figure 5.4 A four-part graphic organizer for Newcomers

Source: Photo of teacher-made graphic organizer for Level 1 Newcomers by Eugenia Krimmel during Millersville University's ESL Clinical Practicum, 2023.

Figure 5.5 Four-part vertical writing organizer

Source: Photo of teacher-made vertical graphic organizer with lines for captions by Eugenia Krimmel during Millersville University's ESL Clinical Practicum, 2023.

how to complete thoughts on their favorite holiday and three reasons why. This high school explanatory task started with discussing, modeling the final product, and drawing on their organizers before filling in words. The Newcomer writing sample in Figure 5.4 shows how the Newcomer used the word wall and modeled examples to write sentences she wanted to express.

The graphic organizer model shown in Figure 5.5 is a four-part vertical organizer with text space used in a sixth-grade writing workshop session about their favorite holiday. Newcomers were familiar with the logic of the information and concepts for this organizer, so the students got right to work. The value of quickly drawing a graphic organizer like two-, three-, and four-part organizers is that ELs or anyone can make their own organizers when tackling a writing assignment or on scrap paper of standardized tests. The skill of planning your writing in whatever language is one of confident writers.

Another example of an effective Level 1 graphic organizer (illustrated in Figure 5.6) is designed for fourth-grade Newcomers to write their main

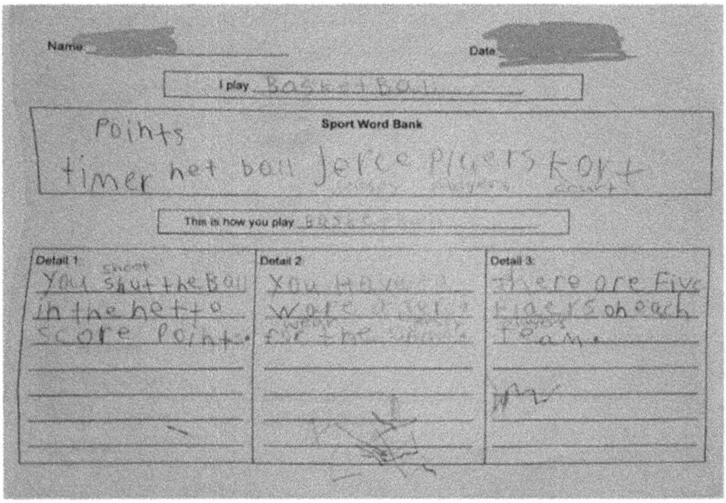

The student above better employed the word bank feature, transferring several content vocabulary words into his writing, such as "court," "jersey," and "players."

Figure 5.6 Explanatory writing task student example

Source: Photo of student-completed Level 1 graphic organizer by Eugenia Krimmel during Millersville University's ESL Clinical Practicum, 2022.

idea and three supporting details for informative or opinion writing tasks. All students benefit from the organization of their ideas, especially basic outlines with sentence starter support for Level 1 and 2 ELs like the blank template in Appendix E. In the example, the writing prompt centers on a favorite sport or game. During the whole class pre-writing activity, students added their own words to the class word wall about sports or games in general. Students then used that word wall to fill in their own personal Sports Word Bank section. Then the Newcomers copied with comprehension from the word wall or from words they learned in English earlier. Each then wrote their three details in complete sentences in the space provided. Help was given as needed. In the student example shown in Figure 5.6, you can see how the Newcomer used new vocabulary words from their own word bank in their sentence writing.

For narrative writing, Newcomers can plan their writing using a simplified graphic organizer (shown in Figure 5.7) to draw their ideas during pre-writing or at the beginning of the writing stage after you model the use

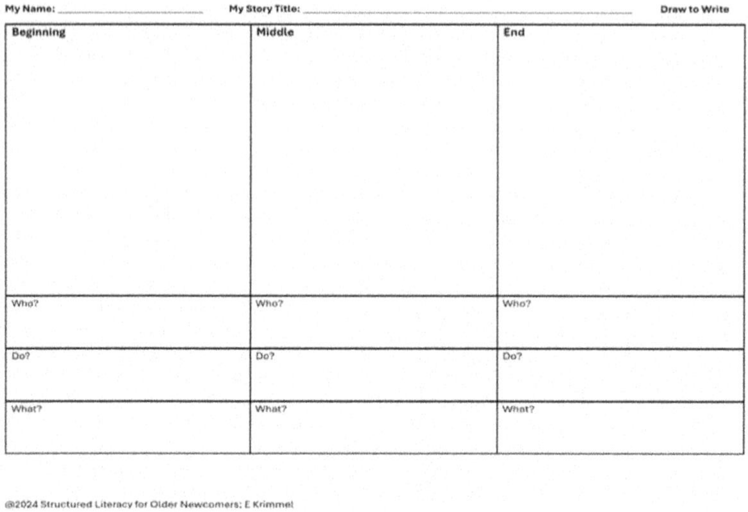

My Name: ________ My Story Title: ________ Draw to Write

Beginning	Middle	End
Who?	Who?	Who?
Do?	Do?	Do?
What?	What?	What?

©2024 Structured Literacy for Older Newcomers; E Krimmel

Figure 5.7 My story organizer

Source: Photo of a teacher-made Level 1 graphic organizer by Eugenia Krimmel during Millersville University's ESL Clinical Practicum, 2024.

of the organizer with the class. A printable copy of this narrative organizer is found in Appendix F to use with the Who? Do? What? writing strategy.

ESL teachers often supply ELs with organizers like the cheeseburger pattern shown in Figure 5.8 to help them write in an English pattern. It is a typical American food and mimics our paragraph organization making it a highly effective visual for teaching English paragraph structure.

Culturally responsive teaching practices respect the fact that there are varying sentence and discourse styles among world languages compared to English (Kaplan, 1966, 1989; Kim & Kozlova, 2020). As can be seen from Figure 5.9, various language groups express their thoughts in differing patterns from English speakers.

Kim and Kozlova conducted research that reinforced Kaplan's (1966) finding that discourse differences between world languages are apparent even in ELs' writing.

> According to the results of the research, based on the material of several languages, these thought patterns of discourse differ considerably across languages. English is characterized by a strict

Parts of a Paragraph

topic sentence
(top bun)

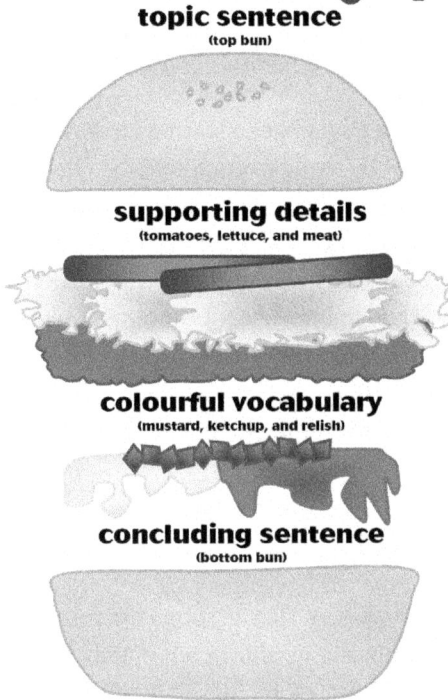

supporting details
(tomatoes, lettuce, and meat)

colourful vocabulary
(mustard, ketchup, and relish)

concluding sentence
(bottom bun)

Figure 5.8 The cheeseburger paragraph graphic organizer

Source: Image of Parts of a Paragraph. Authored by Enokson. Located at: https://flic.kr/p/ak9H3v. License: *CC BY: Attribution.*

Written Discourse Patterns of Language Families

English	Semitic	Sino-Tibetan	Romance	Slavic

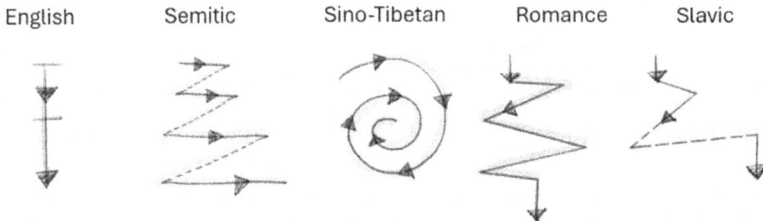

Figure 5.9 Differing language discourse patterns

Source: Created by Eugenia Krimmel based on Kaplan, R. (1966). Cultural thought patterns in intercultural education. *Language Learning, 16*(1), 1–20.

linear structure while Russian written discourse is characterized by a less strictly organized structure [and] numerous digressions from the main topic.

(p. 635)

These differences pose a challenge to learning to write in a new language.

Newcomers may not be ready to complete the cheeseburger organizer, yet. That is still a step beyond their English capabilities as many of the teacher trainees learned during their ESL Specialist clinical practicum using EL Writing Process techniques. These future ESL specialists learned, as you will, that they had to increase the amount of writing asked of Newcomers slowly, so they were not overwhelmed with both language and concept organization. Without this pre-writing step, however, Newcomers often hesitate to write anything at all.

What Are Level 1 Tasks?

Level 1-appropriate materials like graphic organizers build in leveled tasks. Simplified organizers should incrementally increase written production as Newcomers learn more English letters, words, and phrases.

Micro-Writing with Graphic Organizers

Micro-writing or Quick Writes motivate ELs including Newcomers. According to the research on *The Progress Principle* and *The Power of Small Wins* (Amabile & Kramer, 2011), breaking up difficult tasks into micro parts helps the brain perform with more success. Start with small steps and have Newcomers build one letter and then one word within the writing workshops over time. In this pre-writing step, you incorporate micro-writing tasks such as labeling, creating lists, and completing short sentences in graphic organizers. Newcomers can also draw and then label their own images.

Teacher-provided final writing models and template examples show all ELs how to complete organizers if they have never seen one in previous schooling. ELs may not know what is expected of them when given a

Venn diagram or T-chart because this may be new to them. Various executive functioning steps to complete an organizer or a writing task may also not be in place for some ELs. For this reason, model actions of each template or activity. For ELs who enroll later in the school year, assign a buddy or provide a video to show them how to fill in a template. The value of recording thoughts through labels and drawings or images before writing should not be overlooked.

What Does the Pre-Writing Step Look Like in My Class of ELs and Non-ELs?

You differentiate writing tasks for various writing group levels. For example, you are teaching a lesson on written descriptions in Language Arts or extreme weather changes like a hurricane in science.

Have the whole class draw or find an image of a self-driving car or a water-weather event and label the images. Newcomers can at this stage involve their first language and discover the English words by possibly translating them or looking at images to gain understanding. Remember that not all ELs are literate in their first language. Newcomers complete a graphic organizer and sentence starters conveying information about self-driving car safety or describe how a hurricane occurs and how it impacted a family or community using English words as best they can. More advanced English writers and non-ELs could be expected to complete the segmented graphic organizer and write a paragraph independently.

When you plan writing workshop objectives, do not water down the tasks or change to a less critical thinking task. Frame your thoughts around this phrase from Universal Design for Learning (Novak, 2022): Firm Goals, Flexible Means.

To achieve firm goals through flexible means, you will have to scaffold up your writing prompts to help Newcomers understand their assignments. To give you an idea of what this looks like in your class, examples of general education writing prompts found in classes I observed and modified versions with language assistance are provided in Table 5.7. Keep in mind that Newcomers can cognitively do what you ask of their peers. The issue is how much you have to support them as they build their repertoire of English along the way until they can do more on their own. This is where your equity actions come into play in this pre-writing step of the writing process.

Language-Supported Prompts

Provide a language-supported prompt with examples or explanations for clarity of task, required content, and purpose for writing. Add elements to your writing task instructions to give Newcomers a clear idea of the writing task that accompanies the images they will use. Look at the functional language you use in the instructional parts of *product, process, and content* of an assessment. Create language-supported prompts with Newcomers in mind and see how much more writing all your students will produce!

Neither of the examples shown in Table 5.7 supports Newcomers or any learner in their writing tasks. How many of us have seen these typical prompts in a book series? Where do students start? How will they proceed to gather information and organize their writing? Do these prompts provide details about the *content, process, and product* of the task? Rarely.

Because Newcomers understand little to no written English in the beginning, a long, multi-step text-only prompt is not effective, either. However, teachers can present language-supported prompts like the example shown in Table 5.8 for more comprehensible input. Note how the prompt is broken into action steps – the power of small wins, remember?

Table 5.7 Typical General Education Writing Prompt Examples

Example 1: Choose your favorite animal and write interesting facts about it such as where it lives, what it eats, and how it survives in its habitat. Write in complete sentences.
Example 2: Write a summary paragraph about the causes leading to the American Civil War.

Table 5.8 Modified Newcomer Writing Prompt Example

General Education Version with some modification for ELs, but Newcomers need more scaffolding.
You are a bilingual scientist studying the habitat of animals in the world (setting up the purpose of the task).
1. Choose an animal.
2. Describe (1) the habitat or place where it lives (process) in a paragraph (product) including the weather, (2) the food it eats (content), and (3) what is the animal's family group.
3. You help others learn about this animal by writing this information in correct English sentences.
4. Capitalize and add punctuation to your writing.

Example of an ESL Level 1 language-supported prompt:

You are a scientist.

You study animals.

a group of wild animals

1. Choose 1 animal to study *(content)*.
   I want to study _____.
   The following questions address the *process* of the task:
2. Draw and write 1 sentence about where your animal lives (habitat).
   The _____ lives in _____.

Savanna   Tropical Rainforest   Marine

Temperate Forest   Fresh Water   Desert

Grassland   Boreal Forest   Tundra

Draw the weather (climate) and write:

The weather in _____ is _____.

Draw the animal's food. The (animal)_____ eats

_____.

Draw the animal's family. The animal lives in _____ with

_____.

Paragraph Starter (*culminating product*)

Complete the paragraph with the information you have about the animal:

I am a scientist who studies animals. I studied a _____.
    This animal lives _____. The weather in this habitat is
    _____ and the (animal name)_____
    usually eats _____. Animals live in groups. The
    (animal name) _____ lives in a family called a
    _____.

Language-supported writing prompts for Level 1 Newcomers like the example are supported by pictures on the page or a word wall, by a video, or by a short model text. Remember, a language-supported prompt presents the required information (content), step-by-step instructions to complete the task (process), and the culminating writing piece (product) at the end. You supply much of the academic language at this stage while having Newcomers complete the thoughts. Over time you will pull back to a series of sentence starters and then paragraph frames to jumpstart their writing process and build their English writer's confidence.

Say It! Write It! Do It!

Newcomers frequently misunderstand instructions given only verbally, and I have observed countless teachers just talking *at* their students when giving instructions, not helpful for Newcomers and most students. Even with visuals and models, Newcomers may need one-to-one guidance to start and/or to complete a task. Remember to slow down your rate of speech, model with examples, and provide word-level or non-linguistic support when possible.

If a Newcomer is "frozen" or must ask another student what to do, you did not support their language level well enough. Reflect and revise your next steps to ensure better support for your Newcomers. Be sure to communicate with Newcomers in writing, speaking, and showing models.

Technique #2 – Model the Final Writing Product

ELs and MLs, including Newcomers, may come from cultures in which they are not encouraged to produce their own thoughts in academic settings. These students defer to what the teacher tells them to draw or write. In this case, a structured model for creative, persuasive, and/or informative writing helps them have a better idea of how their writing piece should look and what is expected from them.

The use of a final product model in the context of improving students' assignment writing skills is supported by various educational research studies. In 2011, Abbuhl conducted research into the effectiveness of providing finished models or providing models with explicit writing instruction to native English speakers, high-proficiency non-native speakers, and low-proficiency non-native speakers. Abbuhl's study showed the groups receiving models with purposeful, clear-cut writing instruction outperformed those only given models to view. Participants in the study who received the targeted writing instruction along with the final product model commented on how they could identify features in the model which helped them add more to their own writing. Abbuhl's findings also support previous researchers' claims that explicit writing instructions using finalized models need not wait until an EL has reached an advanced level of proficiency (e.g., Ivanič & Camps, 2001; Johns et al., 2006).

Your writing instruction practice should include explicit teaching of the text structure and features of the writing piece. Whether a cause-effect, persuasive, or news article, Hyland (2003) found that ELs of all levels do not include all the features of the final models presented without explicit instruction. Abbuhl's study resulted in a similar trend showing that most ELs do not "get writing by osmosis", but rather they require explicit, systematic, and repeated writing instruction for their own literacy success.

Models of a prompt-to-final product will help you refine how to write prompts for maximum support. You will also find that this helps you prepare a more effective rubric for grading. For example, this middle school science-centered writing prompt asks for facts about a chosen animal:

> *Write an informative paragraph about your favorite animal. Include details about its habitat, diet, or food, and an interesting fact. Use adjectives to describe this interesting animal.*

After reviewing this writing prompt and providing any necessary guidance to find facts, vocabulary, and related adjectives, show students the final model you prepared. Note that the sentences are in simple subject-verb-object format and are written in present tense only. This is the initial level of English syntax or grammar most Newcomers can acquire despite being exposed to more complex English. This is where they generally begin.

Final Product Model – Dolphins

> *Dolphins are cool! They live in oceans all over the world, and they like warm water. Dolphins eat fish and squid. They have <u>sharp</u> teeth to catch their food. Dolphins are very smart. They talk to each other with <u>clicks and whistles</u>. Dolphins are good friends and help each other. They jump out of the water and <u>do tricks</u>. Dolphins are awesome animals!*

Underlined words are an example of the Word Line tool presented in Chapter 6. Basically, a Word Line is a placeholder for words writers are not sure about spelling or if they cannot remember the English word for something they want to say. This is a technique we ask Newcomers to use in the writing step.

Writing Prompt for Tenth-Grade Newcomer ELs

Should children have a limit on screen time? Provide three reasons to support your opinion. Consider the effects on children's bodies, minds, and school success. Use evidence and examples to present that assignment.

Note that the English in the prompt is more complex with the use of "should" and the task requires three to four sentences. Because these Newcomers are in high school, they will encounter more complex English sooner than younger Newcomers. You will have to provide modifications for beginners. Try, for example, changing the prompt question, "Should children have a limit on screen time?" to an opinion question as in the example shown in Table 5.9. This changes the unfamiliar grammatical structure not yet acquired, "should", into a basic present tense question that is more familiar at this early stage of English acquisition.

Table 5.9 Graphic Organizer: Tenth-Grade Writing Prompt

Answer this question with your opinion: Do you agree limits on screen time (watching TV, playing videos, or video games) are good for children? Yes or No? Give three (3) reasons for your opinion. Use descriptions of your ideas.		
Reason 1: Health/body	Reason 2: The mind	Reason 3: School success
EL fills in his/her answer per box to organize their own thoughts. Could draw an image here if time allows or is needed.		

Final Product Model Example

> *It's important to think about how much screen time children have. Screen time means watching TV and playing video games. First, less screen time helps children stay _____ because they can play outside more. Second, it helps children feel less <u>worried</u>. Third, it helps children do better in school because they can focus more. Limiting screen time helps children be happy and successful.*
>
> *(Blank word is "healthy") to be filled in as the teacher presents the final model – class will fill in the Word Line together.*

Once again, this final model is presented in simple sentences that Newcomers can produce at this early stage. The final sentence has a gerund as the subject which will be learned later, but for now, it is a familiar word within the assignment. The final model also models the three reasons required in the prompt. Most of the words are high frequency. Newcomer high schoolers, like all ELs, benefit from the use of high-frequency, familiar words and "concrete words" which are easily shown for comprehension. I encourage you to routinely use a Word Line or two in each final model and demonstrate the use of that tool.

Research on the impact of showing a final model in writing assignments for ELs has been explored by various scholars. Jim Cummins (2007) emphasizes that providing ELs with well-crafted [writing] models can assist them in developing their academic English language skills and understanding the nuances of written English. Showing final models can serve as effective scaffolding, providing a clear example for ELs to follow in their own writing (Gibbons, 2002). Belcher (2012) underscores the role of models in guiding ELs through the conventions of academic writing and helping them navigate the expectations of different genres in academic writing. Providing models of the final writing product benefits all students including ELs and Newcomers during the pre-writing step. The Newcomer writing sample shown in Figure 5.10 demonstrates how much a Newcomer can write in their first draft with sufficient pre-writing instruction such as building background knowledge, modifying materials for better access to the content, and providing a final model so students know what is expected of them.

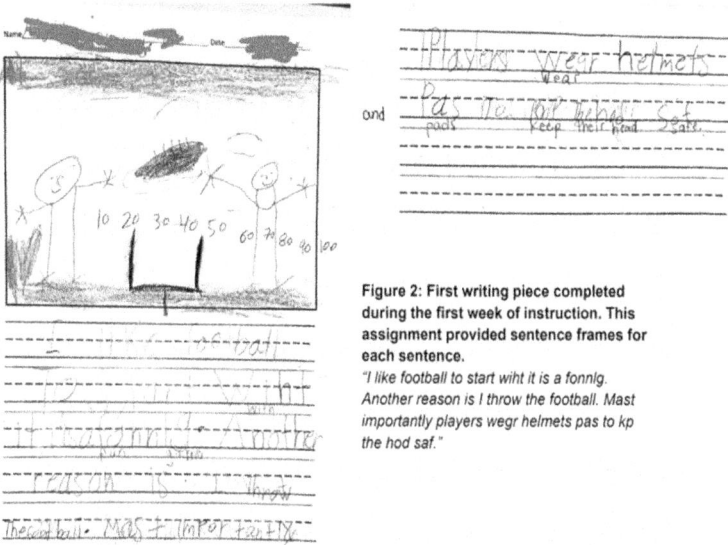

Figure 2: First writing piece completed during the first week of instruction. This assignment provided sentence frames for each sentence.
"I like football to start wiht it is a fonnlg. Another reason is I throw the football. Mast importantly players wegr helmets pas to kp the hod saf."

Figure 5.10 Newcomer sample with Level 1 materials

Source: Photo of the student writing sample using Level 1 material by Eugenia Krimmel during Millersville University's ESL Clinical Practicum, 2022.

ESL Coach's Corner Tips: Pre-writing Step for Newcomers

1. Language-supported prompts designed by teachers like you give Newcomers support to better understand the task and topic of a writing assignment. The pre-writing step is critical to build Newcomers' writing skills and *should not* be a mere five-minute review of a topic and prompt. This step typically takes a writing workshop session or two to complete before having students move on to the writing step.

Pre-writing activities are important for Newcomers' successful writing because they
   a. build new, topic-specific vocabulary.
   b. recall topic-related knowledge and wording in English and/or cognates from their other language(s) from pre-writing texts or visuals.
   c. allow time for planning one's thoughts in their inner speech to prepare what they want to express.
   d. show language patterns at the word, phrase, sentence, and eventually paragraph levels.

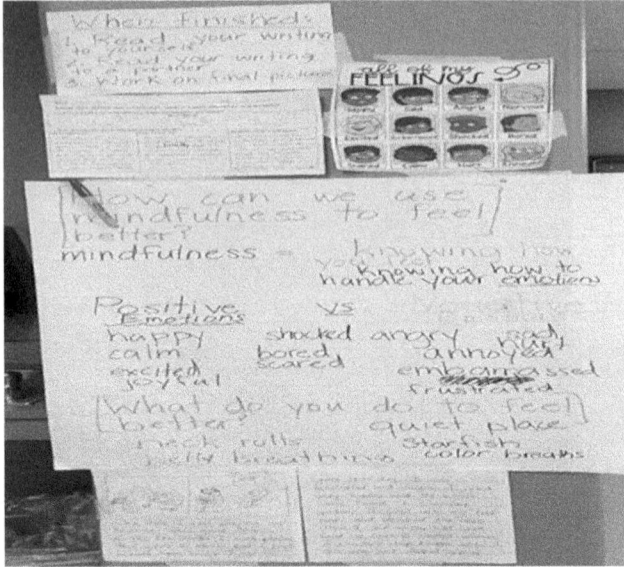

Figure 5.11 Word wall and final product models

Source: Photo of the teacher-made final product example by Eugenia Krimmel during Millersville University's ESL Clinical Practicum, 2022.

    e. provide a model of the writing task (narrative, informative, persuasive, poetry, etc.). Figure 5.11 illustrates all the pre-writing materials you should add to the walls for Newcomers to take in and express lesson-specific ideas in English.

2. Newcomers often looked at these examples during their own writing process. Be sure all reading texts and models are big enough for all students to see from their desks. While training teachers on the EL Writing Process, I have noticed teachers with several held-up notebook papers and reading their final models. How can an EL see that paper as they write? Large chart paper, shared computer screen, or writing on a board that is not erased until after lessons are effective options for modeling the words and written assignments.

3. Do NOT correct spelling during the pre-writing stage. I know you want to do that right away but hold off on the phonics flexing technique which will be explained in Chapter 7. This EL-specific technique is a personalized structured literacy lesson for Newcomers that leads to

accelerated English literacy acquisition. Tell Newcomers not to worry about spelling now and to guess how a word is spelled if not on the word wall or within the mentor text.

4. Try this activity – I observed a couple of teachers doing this activity during pre-writing EL writing time and I believe you will find it useful. To introduce certain letters and sounds of English, give all students a copy of the mentor text in pre-writing. Before reading it, have the students circle "the letter of the day/week". For example, have students circle 5 "A's" or "W's". You can even ask for upper or lower case only. Quickly review the words that contained the letters they circled. Have students call out the words or you call them out. Then ask students to say a word starting with that letter of the day.

From letters, you can progress with this routine activity to word families, prefixes, suffixes, and other morphological parts of words. This is an excellent way to implement structured literacy whether you teach elementary or secondary students. Newcomers will benefit from native English speakers calling out words with those letters or affixes for developing listening skills or what is known as "an English ear".

Reflection Questions:

1. Think about your next writing workshop topic and task. How can you prepare materials and tasks for your Newcomer ELs? Write 3–5 action steps to get your planning started.
2. After a writing workshop cycle is complete, look back at your pre-writing routine, materials, and the tasks Newcomers were asked to complete. What worked and what needs work to help Newcomers be more successful in the next writing workshop?
3. What would you say the reasons are if you had to explain to a colleague why Newcomers need modified materials and tasks during writing workshops?

References

Abbuhl, R. (2011, October–December). Using models in writing instruction: A comparison with native and nonnative speakers of English. *SAGE Open*, *1*(3).

Amabile, T. M., & Kramer, S. J. (2011, May). The power of small wins. *Harvard Business Review, 89*(5).

Belcher, D. (2012). Considering what we know and need to know about second language writing. *Applied Linguistics Review, 3*(1), 131–150.

Collier, V. P., & Thomas, W. P. (1993). How quickly can immigrants become proficient in school English? In *Symposium on bilingual education: Summaries of recent research*. Washington State Institute for Public Policy.

Cummins, J. (1979). Cognitive/academic language proficiency, linguistic interdependence, the optimum age question and some other matters. *Working Papers on Bilingualism, 19*, 121–129.

Cummins, J. (2007). Rethinking monolingual instructional strategies in multilingual classrooms. *Canadian Journal of Applied Linguistics, 10*(2), 221–240.

Elbow, P. (1998). *Writing with power: Techniques for mastering the writing process* (2nd ed.). Oxford University Press.

Gibbons, P. (2002). *Scaffolding language, scaffolding learning: Teaching second language learners in the mainstream classroom*. Heinemann Publishers.

Hyland, K. (2003). *Second language writing*. http://catdir.loc.gov/catdir/samples/cam041/2003041957.pdf

Ivanič, R., & Camps, D. (2001). I am how I sound: Voice as self-representation in L2 writing. *Journal of Second Language Writing, 10*, 3–33.

Johns, A., Bawarshi, A., Coe, R., Hyland, K., Paltridge, B., Rieff, M., & Tardy, C. (2006). Crossing the boundaries of genre studies: Commentaries by experts. *Journal of Second Language Writing, 15*, 234–249.

Kaplan, R. (1966). Cultural thought patterns in intercultural education. *Language Learning, 16*, 1–20.

Kaplan, R. (1989). *Writing in a second language: Contrastive rhetoric. Richness in writing: Empowering esl students* (D. M. Johnson & D. H. Roen, Ed.). Longman Inc.

Kim, L., & Kozlova, L. (2020, April 27–29). Ethnocultural differences in discourse thought patterns and their significance for linguocultural competence. In *10th international conference "word, utterance, text: Cognitive, pragmatic and cultural aspects" (WUT 2020)*. Chelyabinsk State University.

Murray, D. (1972, Fall). *Teach writing as a process not product* (pp. 11–14). The Leaflet/New England Association of Teachers of English.

Nessel, D., & Dixon, C. (2008). *Use the language experience approach with english learners: Strategies for engaging students and developing literacy*. Corwin Press.

Novak, K. (2022). *UDL now! A teacher's guide to applying universal design for learning* (3rd ed.). CAST Publishing.

Sousa, D. A. (2010). *How the ell brain learns*. Corwin Press.

Wilber, S., & Sullivan, F. (2016). *Keys to great writing revised and expanded: Mastering the elements of composition and revision* (2nd ed.). Writer's Digest Books.

6 The Writing Step

Overview of the Writing Step

The writing stage, also known as the drafting or composing stage, is the phase in the writing process where the writer puts their ideas into a visual form to share with others. This is when the initial thoughts and plans generated during the pre-writing stage are organized into a first draft.

Allow yourself the freedom of an imperfect first draft (Wilber & Sullivan, 2016). Hemingway was fond of saying, "The only thing that matters about your first draft is that you finish it". In other words, just write. Give yourself the benefit of sketching out a draft that is nothing more than a beginning. Once you created a text, you can always go back and rewrite and polish and fuss over it. The idea is to "get it written, not right".

EL-Integrated Technique #3 – Draw-to-Draft

Why Is Drawing Before Drafting Important for Newcomers?

Drawing before drafting essays can be a valuable and effective strategy for Newcomers and most ELs entering academic settings. This approach taps into visual and spatial processing, providing learners with a creative and structured way to organize their thoughts. Here are some key reasons why drawing can be beneficial for Newcomers and all ELs before they start drafting essays:

DOI: 10.4324/9781003610595-9

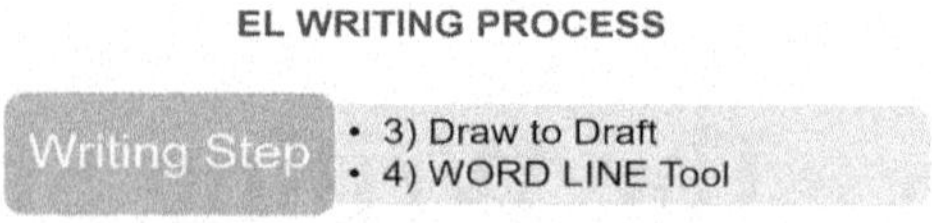

EL WRITING PROCESS

Writing Step
- 3) Draw to Draft
- 4) WORD LINE Tool

Image 6.a EL writing process writing step

1. Visual Organization

   Drawing allows ELs to visually organize their ideas. This visual representation can serve as a roadmap of what they want to convey before turning their thoughts into written form.

2. Building Vocabulary

   Drawing provides an opportunity for ELs to reinforce and expand their vocabulary. As they sketch or label elements of their visual representation, they can practice using relevant academic vocabulary. This not only enhances their language skills but can also enhance their word choice when they begin writing.

3. Reducing Anxiety

   For most people, including ELs, the blank page can be intimidating, leading to anxiety and writer's block. Drawing serves as a low-pressure, creative activity that allows them to ease into the writing process. It creates a comfortable starting point and helps build confidence before transitioning to the more formal structure of word or sentence writing.

4. Clarifying Ideas

   Drawing helps ELs clarify their thoughts and refine their arguments. The act of visually representing ideas forces them to think critically about the relationships between concepts they want to convey and the written English forms. Newcomers can use either their own drawing or an image they found to visualize their language expression.

5. Enhancing Communication Skills

   Drawing promotes communication skills by encouraging Newcomers and ELs to think about how they will convey their ideas visually and then translate them into written English. This dual process reinforces both their visual and verbal communication abilities, essential skills for academic success. In other words, the draw-to-draft technique allows Newcomers to mentally envision what they want to communicate, giving them a feeling of empowerment over the typical silence they feel at this stage.

6. Catering to Different Learning Styles

   ELs come from diverse backgrounds and have varied learning styles. Some may be visual learners who benefit significantly from visual aids. Drawing accommodates those with visual and tactile learning preferences, making the learning experience more personalized and effective. This draw-to-draft approach acknowledges the diversity of learning styles among ELs and non-ELs to foster a more inclusive and supportive academic environment.

Time for Images

Why start writing by drawing or finding images? This technique provides Newcomers with a creative and low-pressure entry point into the writing process. Based on the pre-writing step activities, Newcomers were shown how to create or curate an image for the writing workshop topic. Many ELs may feel hesitant to write because they lack confidence in English writing. To lower their anxiety, have them draw their thoughts first. Making pictures is often more enjoyable than writing for some students but not all. We found some Newcomers attempted to write words before drawing. Either way the aim is getting thoughts on paper.

Checklist for image time:

- Using any graphic organizers from the pre-writing step and having students start to draw or find images to express their ideas.
- Paper with an area to draw or paste an image at the top with lined or double-lined paper below the open space as appropriate depending on the age of Newcomers. Blank paper will do as well but writing may be unevenly spaced.
- Pencils, erasers, crayons, colored pencils, or glue sticks for pasting images from magazines or printout should be made available during drawing-to-draft time.
- Digital platforms such as BookCreator, ClassKick, PowerPoint slides, or a digital whiteboard so that the author can take a screenshot can also be used for this activity. Even Word or Google Docs can be used for digital expression of thoughts. Various tools like digital-colored pens allow Newcomers to create their visual ideas online.

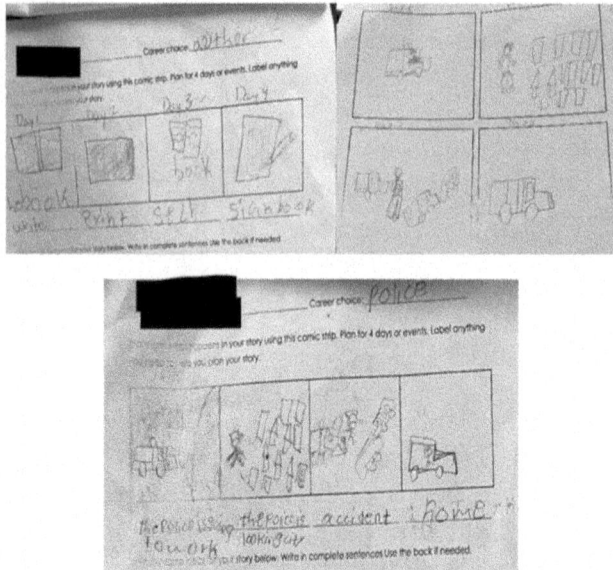

Figure 6.1 Newcomer draw-to-draft samples

Source: Photo of student writing samples of draw-to-draft activity by Eugenia Krimmel during Millersville University's ESL Clinical Practicum, 2023.

- Direct students who finished their images to begin writing based on their organizer or image to complete the writing step. Figure 6.1 illustrates Newcomer draw-to-draft examples.

Time for Writing

Your Newcomers are finally ready to write letters, words, or phrases based on their linguistic readiness and their thoughts. Keep in mind that because Newcomers have a limited ability at this stage to produce much English writing, a 10-to-15-minute session should be sufficient for them to produce their thoughts in the written word (whether English or their first language). Look beyond the mechanics of writing in this step and encourage Newcomers to write as much as they can even if that is copying with comprehension from the word wall. Time given to Newcomers for sustained silent writing has shown significant improvements in writing scores and student-assessed writing confidence levels according to researchers Fahmi Bin Fo'att et al. (2018).

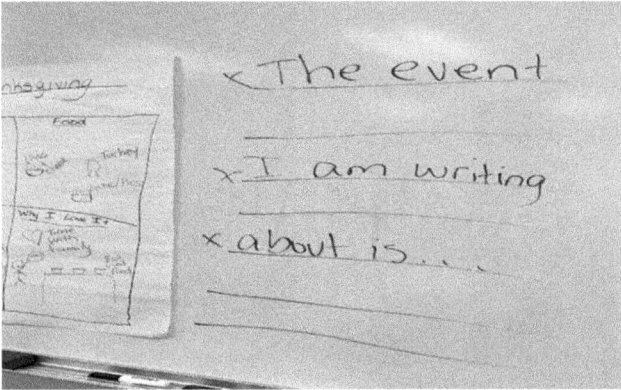

Figure 6.2 Spacing of writing example

Source: Photo of the teacher-made example of skipping lines while writing during the teacher underwriting step by Eugenia Krimmel during Millersville University's ESL Clinical Practicum, 2023.

By engaging with their own thoughts, Newcomers' self-to-text connections allow for enhanced comprehension when learning how to write their words in English. This attempt to write in English is an invaluable step toward writing fluency and is not a dead-end copy-without-comprehension task so often assigned to Newcomers from day one of classroom lessons. Your instruction for all students is geared toward writing to learn; therefore, these techniques boost that opportunity.

In addition to graphic organizers for drawing, you should instruct your students to write by skipping every other line or somehow leaving space for feedback. Elementary grades often have specialized writing paper that has this spacing, but giving notebook paper to older students means you have to show them what "skip every other line" means. Figure 6.2 illustrates what it looks like in a classroom setting. Appendix G supplies a blank example of skipping lines to show your Newcomers. A digital version of this skip line graphic organizer is also found in the Support Materials folder.

Word Walls for Copying with Comprehension

Remind Newcomers to use the word or language phrase walls (physical or digital) in their writing. They should choose to copy the words they

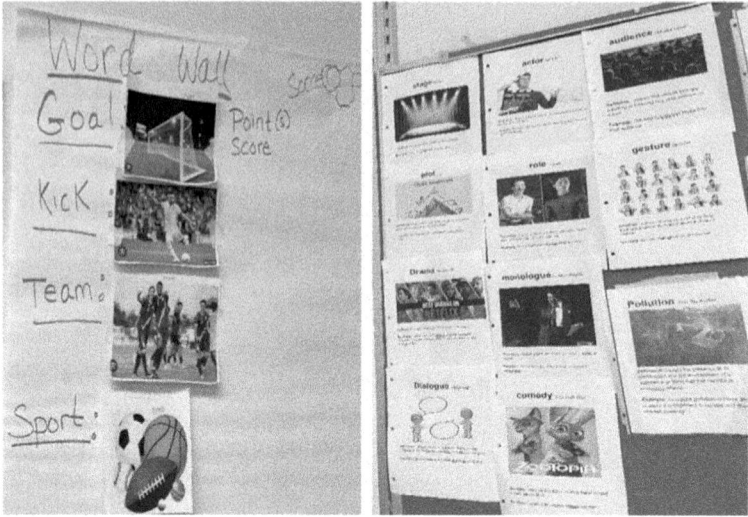

Figure 6.3 Level 1 word walls with images

Photo of teacher-made word walls with images for Newcomers by Eugenia Krimmel during Millersville University's ESL Clinical Practicum, 2023.

comprehend to express their ideas. In the pre-writing step, lesson-specific words were added to an existing word wall or form a new topic-specific word/phrase wall, as shown in Figure 6.3. When Newcomers use this resource to write, they copy words they comprehend – words they intentionally want to use in their writing.

This is valuable in the SLA process because Newcomers recognize the words, have a mental image, and now use it to express their own thoughts. The words or phrases they copy are more deeply internalized for future recall. *Copying with comprehension* is a critical starting point that leads to decoding and encoding for meaningful written expression.

What Is Translanguaging?

Translanguaging is a theory that multilingual people, including Newcomers, have a broader repertoire of linguistic systems in their minds that they use to make sense of their world and express their thoughts. This integration of languages is known as *translanguaging*. This is NOT translation (Otheguy et al., 2015).

Example Scenario:

> When I (Eugenia) was a high school exchange student to Turkey, I knew no Turkish upon arrival. My host family spoke no English. We had a bit of trouble communicating at first. My host father finally asked me in French if I was hungry or thirsty. Breakthrough! I had had four years of French in high school and understood what he asked despite his Turkish accent on his French. I used not my native language, but another language I had learned to make sense of my world in that moment. I relied on the knowledge stored in my wider linguistic repertoire to interact and understand what my host father was saying. I also recalled my knowledge of French to respond to him so that he could understand me – Translanguaging in action.

Whether interacting with people or writing text, Newcomers should be encouraged to and afforded opportunities to use all their cognitive assets. Translanguaging should be a routine practice of educational equity for MLs in your classroom. You may be thinking, "Isn't English the goal?". Yes, of course, but to deny or encourage a student not to use all their assets defeats equity for all. Teachers should provide ways and means for Newcomers to transfer their thoughts into English eventually, but at first thoughts-to-paper is the task.

Translanguaging in the Writing Process

Translanguaging opportunity – Encourage Newcomers to get their thoughts on paper in whatever language they wish at first. If Newcomers use their first language, encourage them to find the translation into English when finished writing the first draft because the goal is the skill of writing in English as an *additional* language to add to their linguistic repertoire. We are not replacing their first language. This act of seeking translation whether by electronic translation or by asking someone who knows their language also assists the brain to internalize words better than if simply given the translated text.

Although you can provide Newcomers bilingual resources like a word-to-word bilingual dictionary or digital translation app, make them write what they can in English first. Force their recall of what was presented in the pre-writing step because they should be thinking in English as much as their proficiency allows at any given moment. Then when needed, they can turn to translation resources. In time those tools will no longer be necessary and even become tiresome as Newcomers improve their English proficiency. The key here is to facilitate Newcomers' need to find their words in English, so do not translate for them unless you are the only other means of learning those words. Do not just give them the English words at this point.

As a teacher of Newcomers, you will add opportunities to use translanguaging as a way to celebrate diversity in your classroom that builds a sense of belonging. As an assets-based, culturally sustaining pedagogical practice, expect Newcomers to use translanguaging to acquire and express their ideas because they do not have enough English vocabulary or patterns in their heads, yet. You should encourage Newcomers to use all their resources to enhance their thought-to-writing skill development.

For example, a child may write "mi hermana sits in a silla" alongside a picture of a girl in a chair. This Newcomer is using all her linguistic assets to communicate her thoughts. During individual and/or small-group instruction, you will write under the child's sentence, "My sister sits in a chair". The Newcomer will now make the connection between her written thoughts and the way these are written in English. This process moves Newcomers one step closer to more fluent English writing.

SLA research suggests that when target language input goes in, the brain tries to associate that input with something familiar so that it will not slip away from the short-term memory (Sousa, 2010). Herein lies the reason EL writing techniques accelerate Newcomer's literacy development skills. Because the Newcomer's own thoughts are on the paper, the written English they wrote is more readily connected to their own ideas rather than the text from a random book or even from peers' writing. Using EL writing techniques, teachers can also consolidate Newcomers integrated English language skill development with great effect. Using their own thoughts as the basis, they facilitate both content and language learning.

The assets-based viewpoint of the EL Writing Process is based on the principle of LEA that incorporates student's knowledge of the world, languages, and social interactions into instructional material for learning. LEA coupled with translanguaging opportunities allow Newcomers to express their thoughts on paper in English from day one even if only a letter or a word is produced. Approaching literacy instruction from both the basic forms and comprehension perspectives at the same time empowers Newcomers as they develop into fluent academic English writers.

EL-Integrated Technique #4 – Word Line Tool

The Power of a Placeholder

A placeholder in the writing process is one of the most valuable tools to prevent getting stuck or frozen in thought. In the world of writing, a placeholder is a temporary stand-in that reserves a space in a sentence while writing. Later the writer fills in the space to complete the sentence. The main idea is to keep the structure and grammar of a sentence or text in place but still have the freedom to switch up the words later.

Novelists and movie script writers use placeholders, so they are not bogged down by thoughts of which word to use or how to spell something (Doctorow, 2009). A well-known example of placeholder use in writing was publicized when *Star Trek: The Next Generation* writer Ron Moore revealed that they used the word "tech" when they could not think of a word right away but wanted to get their thoughts on paper. An excerpt of a script from the show looks like this:

La Forge: "Captain, the tech is overteching".
Picard: "Well, route the auxiliary tech to the tech, Mr. La Forge".
La Forge: "No, Captain. Captain, I've tried to tech the tech, and it won't work".
Picard: "Well, then we're doomed".
"And then Data pops up and says, 'Captain, there is a theory that if you tech the other tech . . .'".

Source: https://forum.quartertothree.com/t/ive-tried-to-tech-the-tech-ron-moore-and-placeholder-tech/55327

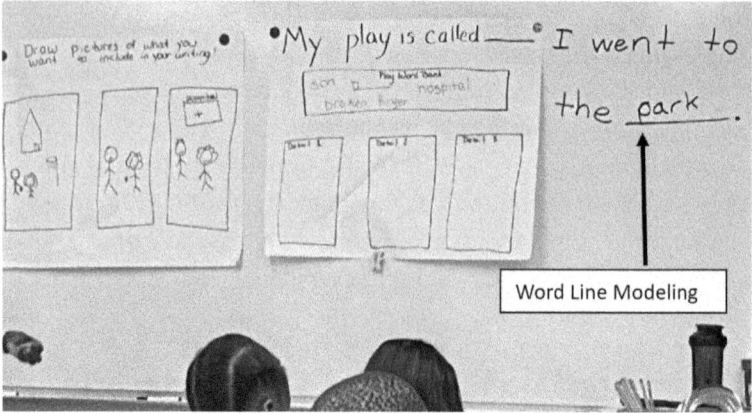

Figure 6.4 Teacher model of the Word Line writer's tool

Source: Photo of the teacher-made model of Word Line use by Eugenia Krimmel during Millersville University's ESL Clinical Practicum, 2023.

If brilliant writers like Moore benefit from using placeholders, then Newcomers will benefit, too. Unlike movie writers using an English word, a word line is a lined space either blank or under an attempted word spelling that Newcomers can draw for words they cannot spell or recall when they are writing. Writers go back later to fill in the line with the correct word or spelling. As mentioned in the pre-writing's final model technique, model the use of a word line in the pre-writing step by going through the thought process of why you drew the word line in your final written model text. Did you draw a word line because you are not sure which word you should write, or you did not know how to spell it? Talk that through so Newcomers will apply this tool in their own writing.

Keep in mind that Newcomers whose first language includes gender markers such as Spanish (*el* chico or *la* chica) may add a word line for these words. Through TU's assets-based error correction and improved proficiency over time, Newcomers will stop using this "extra line". Figure 6.4 shows the teacher model of the Word Line tool and Figure 6.5 displays student use of the Word Line tool in the first draft.

Another example of the final model including a Word Line is illustrated in Figure 6.6 based on a third-grade science standard-based prompt to explain the life cycle of a frog. The teacher offers his written paragraph while showing students how to incorporate the Word Line strategy. You

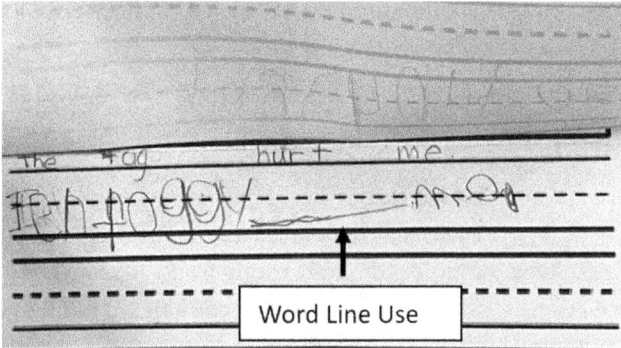

Figure 6.5 Student use of the Word Line writer's tool

Source: Photo of the student writing sample by Eugenia Krimmel during Millersville University's ESL Clinical Practicum, 2022.

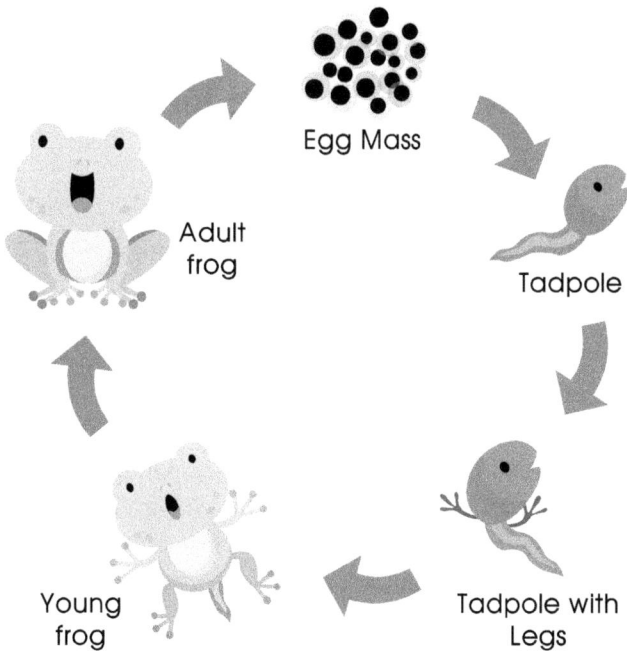

Figure 6.6 Final model with Word Line modeling

will have to model this often until it becomes a routine tool all your student writers can use when writing fluently.

Final Model:

> My favorite animal is a frog. I like frogs because they jump and eat _____. Their eggs turn into baby tadpoles and then they grow legs. Next, tadpoles turn into young frogs. At last young frogs become a _____ (loud or noisy?) adult frog. I think frogs are fun and happy animals.

Some Newcomers learn text messaging in the course of arrival to U.S. schools and interacting with English speakers. Do not allow students to write in acronyms or "text message spellings"; instead have them write out each word. The word I saw most often among Newcomers was "cuz" for "because". They do not realize the error because they hear many peers say "cuz" when speaking instead of "because", so you may have to show them these words specifically as they appear.

Coach's Corner: Writing Step for Newcomers

1. Suggested routine for drawing activity instructions
   After modeling the final product with a word line and spacing every other line on paper, instruct your students to
   - think about the topic again.
   - review their graphic organizer, word walls, and class discussions notes.
   - draw images until you hear the timer sound (*Note:* I highly suggest you limit their drawing time, or some will continue to draw or color).
   - use 3 colors in their drawings. (If it is a narrative writing assignment, you can suggest using blue for characters, red for actions, and green for settings, for example. If it is an argumentative or expository task, assign colors to the parts of each text structure: blue for claim, red for supporting ideas, and green for counterclaim, for example.) Color activates creativity in the brain, so it is good for this stage of thinking to write.

You may have to remind them not to copy your final model. I also observed Newcomers writing "WORD BANK" on their drawings as if that was a vocabulary term they should include in their drawing labels. Consider eliminating the WORD WALL term and just give lists or put lesson-specific words on a colored poster or a particular wall in the room. They will learn what that list is quite quickly as you point and refer to it often.

2. Do not collect their writing assignments for error correction at this point: Teachers are known to collect written papers and correct them at a later time. All my school years teachers did error corrections that way. It was totally disconnected. Correction without conferencing is less effective particularly with Newcomers because you may not know what they wrote and was trying to say. This is a missed opportunity not to have a one-to-one quick conference. As you will see in the next chapter, conferencing with bilingual writers is key to improving their phonics, spelling, and writing proficiency in English.

If you collect their writing at this stage of the writing process, do so to inform your mini lesson plans within that writing workshop unit, but not to correct grammar and spelling. I used to do this very thing because that was what I saw my teachers do. I handed back reddened writing assignments, and the students could care less about revisions or improvements. I learned over my many years of teaching ELs writing that this is skill development and requires constant guidance for one student at a time, and I found the time to do error correction more effectively by reviewing with each.

3. Scripts and Keyboards

An important aspect to keep in mind in this step of the writing process is how well Newcomers can write or keyboard in the English (Latin-based) script. ELLs from Arabic, Chinese, and Russian language groups, for example, may be learning the alphabet while tackling word-level writing. If your ELLs are keyboarding, they may have never used an English keyboard. Having ELLs write even on day one of class will give them opportunities to develop these skills that are essential to communicating their thoughts in both academic and social settings. Newcomers may however take a bit longer to complete writing in this stage of acquisition. Examples

Figure 6.7 Examples of different world language alphabets

of the English alphabet should also be readily available for all ELLs, especially for those whose first language uses a non-Latin script.

Recording one's thoughts in this modern era can be done on paper or digitally. Both can be tricky for Newcomers. Handwriting involves the written script differences in symbols, directionality, and even punctuation markings. The Omniglot.com website provides information about hundreds of languages that most of your Newcomers know. That is a good starting place to learn about the writing systems and alphabets your Newcomers have to crossover to learn English. Figure 6.7 shows the many alphabets most languages use in our modern times. For those ELs learning handwriting, specific letter formations and directionality should be checked and addressed periodically in mini lessons or individual practice activities.

Ideally ELs should master both systems of recording their thoughts in writing in their first and additional languages. Younger students normally learn to write on paper and practice handwriting; however, even kindergarten students who attend cyber schools use a keyboard for writing. Newcomers may benefit from *Handwriting or Keyboarding Without Tears*-type practice programs in the younger grades while NALA's Better-Handwriting-For-Adults program will appeal to your older Newcomers.

Did you know a British English keyboard varies from an American keyboard's arrangement of keys? Other language keyboards are completely different even if using a Latin script; therefore, providing Newcomers with

Figure 6.8 Turkish language keyboard

web-based keyboarding games or programs like *Keyboarding Without Tears* will help them learn to write digitally with ease over time. Figure 6.8 shows you what a Turkish keyboard looks like. Now imagine having to write a paper on a computer with this arrangement of letters. It will slow you down just as it does for many Els and MLs. Speaking in English is one skill, but writing and keyboarding in English is quite another skill.

Integration of writing step EL techniques draw-to-draft and the Word Line tool into your writing workshop practice offers Newcomers an opportunity to

1. organize their thoughts visually before tackling the difficult task of writing in a new language.
2. use new vocabulary words in their writing to express their own thoughts.
3. avoid typical writer's block of second language writers by employing a Word Line placeholder to fill in later during TU time or when the word comes to mind.

Reflection Questions:

1. How can you encourage Newcomers to draw what they want to express if they are hesitant to draw anything?
2. What role do you believe a Newcomer's first language plays in your writing workshop process?
3. How does the Word Line tool help Newcomers accelerate their literacy skills in English?
4. When ca n you switch instructions from draw-to-draft to draft-to-draw and why?

References

Doctorow, C. (2009, January 5). Writing in the age of distraction. *Locus Journal*, *62*(1). https://www.locusmag.com/Features/2009/01/cory-doctorow-writing-in-age-of.html

Fahmi Bin Fo'att, M., Wah Li Ting, F., & Wong Shi-Lei, C. (2018, June). The effects of sustained silent writing on the writing scores and perception of writing confidence and competence of primary 5 students. *ELIS Classroom Inquiry*. https://academyofsingaporeteachers.moe.edu.sg/docs/librariesprovider2/resouces-docs/elis-research-fund-reports/2018-xingnan.pdf

Otheguy, R., García, O., & Reid, W. (2015). Clarifying translanguaging and deconstructing named languages: A perspective from linguistics. *Applied Linguistics Review*, *6*(3), 281–307.

Sousa, D. A. (2010). *How the ell brain learns*. Corwin Press.

Wilber, S., & Sullivan, F. (2016). *Keys to great writing revised and expanded: Mastering the elements of composition and revision* (2nd ed.). Writer's Digest Books.

7 Edit and Revision Step

Overview of Editing

Editing stage is a crucial step in the writing process. Its focus is on refining the coded message of a written piece to ensure intended communication. Editing involves both macro-level concerns, such as structure and organization, and micro-level details, such as sentence-level word choice, spelling, and grammar errors. During this stage, writers review and make changes to improve the clarity, coherence, grammar, syntax, and overall effectiveness of their writing.

Overview of Revising

The revision stage is an equally crucial part of the writing process, where writers review, modify, and refine their drafts to improve or expand their intended message. During revision, writers often focus on content organization, structure, and style to ensure that their thoughts are effectively communicated.

Edit and Revise with Newcomers

Newcomers connect to micro-level editing more readily because it usually centers on letters and words. Revision for Newcomers will mostly take place as rewriting teacher underwriting corrections in their beginner

DOI: 10.4324/9781003610595-10

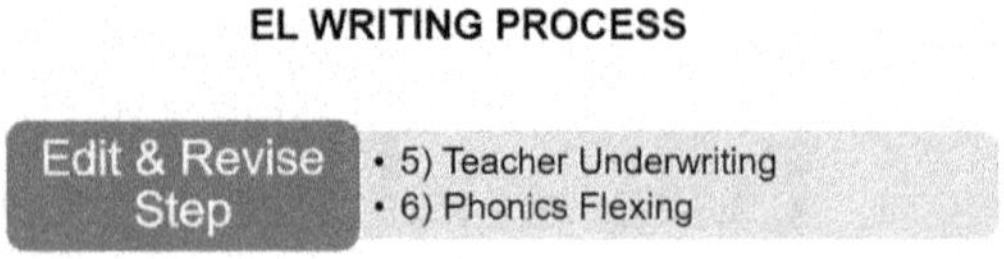

EL WRITING PROCESS

Edit & Revise Step	• 5) Teacher Underwriting • 6) Phonics Flexing

Image 7.a EL writing edit and revise step

stage. With effective literacy instruction and exposure to accessible reading passages, Newcomers will begin revising as soon as they are ready.

The macro-level editing and revising will advance as Newcomers' English proficiency increases, but initially getting their thoughts on paper through correct phonics, spelling, and word choice is the aim of the EL Writing Process. Keep in mind writing is thinking, and Newcomers can think to the level of their peers. We teachers are tasked with helping them communicate those thoughts in writing.

As educators, we hold a pivotal role in shaping the language learning journey of our Newcomer ELs. In this chapter, we delve into the essence of why teachers should actively engage in the editing and revising process of their students' initial drafts. Chang (2016) advocates for educators to view errors not as setbacks but as teachable moments. He contends that teachers like you and me can transform English "mishaps" into opportunities for literacy skill growth. Tanaka (2010) stresses the cultural dimension embedded in language and encourages teachers to engage actively in the editing process. Tanaka suggests that teachers, by editing with a culturally informed lens, bridge the gap between students' native language nuances and those of the English language.

Ramirez and Jones (2013) indicate that by actively participating in the editing process, teachers empower students to take ownership of their English expression while fostering positive confidence in their albeit limited ability to learn the new language. In a nutshell, researchers imply it is an advantage to Newcomers and their English literacy development to routinely incorporate one-to-one editing and revising in your writing workshop practice. While you and I may agree with these researchers in theory, what does that look like during your writing workshop time? This is the point in the EL Writing Process that two EL techniques truly impact Newcomers' literacy skills: teacher underwriting and phonics flexing.

Table 7.1 Teacher Underwriting and Phonics Flexing

Teacher Underwriting	Revision Step	Reviews overall writing: addresses read-aloud syntax errors like word order and omitted words; marks misspellings
Phonics Flexing	Editing Step	Focuses on misspellings only through a speech-to-text, whole-part-whole approach to spelling correction and connecting the phoneme sounds to letters in English

Revision, altering contextual content for added or different thoughts, can happen when rewriting, but it is not encouraged in the EL Writing Process for Newcomers. One reason is that it most likely took a longer time for them to produce a text compared to their peers, so revising the new writing piece is too time-consuming. Another reason is you will want to review it and give feedback which will also take time in your already busy curriculum calendar.

To help you better visualize the relationship of TU to PF within the EL Writing Process, Table 7.1 shows how TU aligns with revision while PF intersects with the editing step. What will become apparent to you is how you will combine both TU and PF into one step in the writing process instead of separating editing and revising as with non-ELs. You will perform these two EL techniques together seamlessly in one-to-one conferencing with each Newcomer.

EL-Integrated Technique #5 – Teacher Underwriting

Now that you have set up the writing topic and made it accessible to Newcomers through Level 1 materials, showing final models, and giving students time to draw-to-draft with the Word Line tool as an option, it is time for personalized error correction and structured literacy instruction in the form of editing and revising. Newcomers require explicit literacy instruction to reach their near-peer level of English reading and writing as quickly as possible; therefore, personalized instructional feedback on their own authentic text impacts their internalization of sounds, letters, and word patterns in this new language. The EL technique of TU activates Newcomers' learning process through teacher modeling and conscientious-raising (C-R) actions that assist the bilingual brain in acquiring English language patterns more deeply. Consciousness-raising is defined as "the deliberate attempt to draw the learner's attention specifically to the formal properties of the target language" (Rutherford & Sharwood Smith, 1985, p. 274).

Consciousness-raising techniques are pivotal in second language learning because they foster active participation and deeper understanding. Through guided discovery, error analysis, and explicit instruction, learners reflect on language use, enhancing accuracy, fluency, and communicative competence. This book's EL Writing Process techniques offer practical activities for incorporating C-R strategies into your teaching practice to facilitate effective language learning and learner autonomy.

Teacher underwriting is the action of re-reading and rewriting under or near the student's original writing in correct, fluent English while reviewing the written piece with the student author. See Figure 7.1 to visualize what TU looks like on paper.

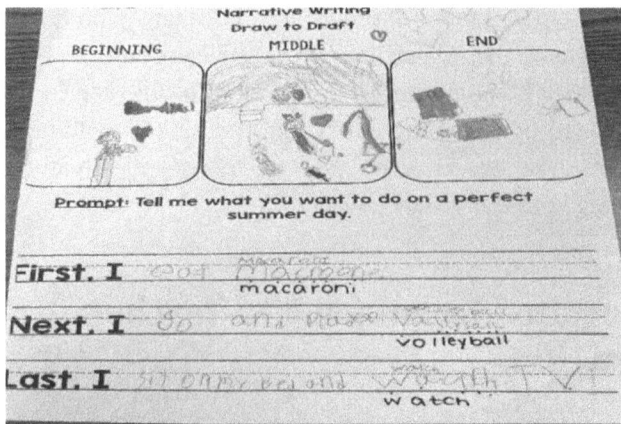

Figure 7.1 Teacher underwriting example

Source: Photo of the student writing sample after teacher underwriting by Eugenia Krimmel during Millersville University's ESL Clinical Practicum, 2022.

TU begins with the student reading back what she or he wrote to reinforce their writing and receive personalized feedback. If there are no errors in spelling or syntax, TU is not necessary. This may happen if they simply copy your final model or copy from another text source. You can prevent that from happening in the pre-writing stage with the materials and tasks you present; however, sometimes Newcomers only copy because they may not have understood the task, or they want their writing to be perfect. In this case, judge your timing to see if you can have them attempt another draft or let it go, and be careful in the next writing workshop to eliminate copying of whole text as mentioned in Chapter 5 and the pre-writing stage.

If a Newcomer's writing does include errors, you will underwrite their words or help fill in the <u>word lines</u> used as placeholders as you hear your EL read back his or her piece. If there is a home language word written within their text, talk about the word with the Newcomer and write it in English under their word. If possible, have the Newcomer translate the word themselves so the brain has to work for that knowledge. This is a best practice of SLA which should raise their consciousness to the correlation between the first language word and the English word. Some Newcomers may even misspell a word in their first language.

Reasons why some Newcomers do not read or write in their native language can be a lack of schooling due to gender, poverty, war, or students' medical issues. Inadequate literacy instruction may also be a reason and result in poor literacy skills or even mask an undetected special need like dyslexia. You may not know whether your Newcomers are unable to write in their native language at first. You can ask them to write a sentence describing their favorite food or a "would you rather" statement in their own language as a quick test.

Native language writing forms the basis for Newcomers' knowledge of thoughts in print but if that is missing, they will learn that concept in English only. Remember that translation is not the best action to take when Newcomers are struggling. Show not tell as often as you can using gestures, visuals, and modeling to communicate is an acquisition best practice. Encourage your Newcomers to do the same – show you what they are trying to say.

What Does Teacher Underwriting Look Like?

The TU technique happens during the readback activity with a student whether individually or when you focus on their writing in a small group. Figure 7.2 illustrates the use of TU to provide personalized literacy instruction and error correction to Newcomers after they draw and write their ideas.

Each teacher may conduct their writing workshop slightly differently depending on timing and student needs. However, these are the steps recommended for effective TU with Newcomers in only EL or mixed EL and non-EL groups:

Step 1: After Newcomers write or label their drawings, you will place them in small groups. You review one piece at a time from within the small group. Perform TU to provide personalized feedback to an individual student author while the others observe – and learn! All the other group members benefit from watching and listening. Or you can work with one Newcomer at a time individually if preferred.

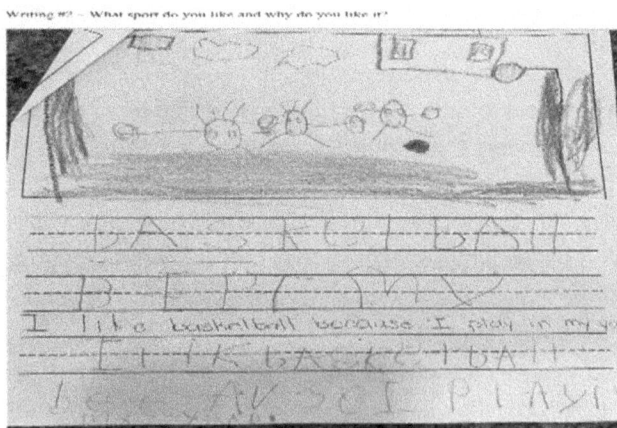

Figure 7.2 Teacher underwriting in response to a prompt

Source: Photo of the teaching underwriting example on student writing by Eugenia Krimmel during Millersville University's ESL Clinical Practicum, 2022.

Step 2: Proceed with the TU technique by reviewing the image drawn or found by your Newcomer author. Keep in mind that beyond Level 1, even EL writers will not need TU and PF as much. It is a gradual release from this technique toward your routine writing feedback procedure, however, in this initial stage technique.

Next, ask the student author to read their writing to you. Do not read it to them because that defeats the purpose of this step. You want to know what they *know*; what they *can write and read* at this early stage. Allow the student to finish each sentence or the whole writing piece before going back to point out corrections. Level 1 Newcomers do not write much generally, so the time to review any corrections is minimal.

Step 3: Teacher Underwriting Notation: During the TU review process, you stop at any misspelled words and put a dot or zigzag line under it before you perform the PF technique which is described below. You continue choral reading with the student author to the next word requiring attention if any. For example, if the Newcomer has written this sentence, you can put a dot or zigzag line under the word to highlight that it needs attention.

If a student author adds a spoken word not in their writing during the choral readback, add that to the TU using an arrow or line to indicate where that word should be within the flow of the sentence. When Newcomers add words while re-reading, they give the teacher insight into words they have internalized orally but not yet in writing. Jot down notes when you can to log these "mishaps" in their writing. Typically, Newcomers omit prepositions and articles because these may not exist in their first language, so these are typical errors to record.

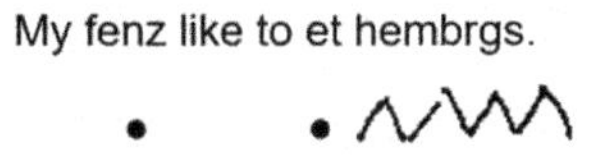

My fenz like to et hembrgs.

Image 7.b Image of teacher underwriting symbols

What If the Newcomer Cannot or Will Not Read It Back to You?

You should insist on reading it together in a choral read-type action. If a student author mostly copies words without comprehension, this hesitancy to read back may happen. Be patient and read slowly with them to give Newcomers time to process the sound-letter patterns. Continue with the process of corrections and PF as the need arises.

Step 4: You can also ask the student author about any word lines in their writing. Write what the word lines are meant to represent when underwriting as the student reads from their writing piece. You can write that word on the word line as if the student wrote it there originally. Newcomers will see those words in written form, and each will be highlighted for consciousness-raising in their bilingual brain.

Step 5: At the end of the TU process, praise the Newcomer's accuracy and logical approximations of English sound-symbol relationships by saying something like "Nice writing" or "I see your ideas in your writing".

In the writing step, if you remember, you showed your students how to write on every other line or space out their words. This is important because you have plenty of room to perform TU and PF. You will have to model this spacing several times. In addition, you will model how Newcomers will turn the first draft and personalized corrections into a more polished final draft. This will be addressed in more detail in Chapter 8 on the Publishing step.

Should I Underwrite Every Word or Only Those Misspelled or Missing?

That is your call. You know your Newcomers best, but consider these guidelines to help you make that decision:

1. Number of Corrections – Knowing that Newcomers' independent English writing is very limited, they may only write a letter, a word, or a short sentence. If this is the case, you should correct all their errors. With longer pieces, you can limit the number of underwriting words, so you do not overwhelm Newcomers' bilingual brains. You may want to use what I call the "Power of Three" which means only pointing out three types of errors if there are quite a few misspellings or omissions.

You may choose to underwrite only three misspelled words per writing piece. Or you may feel it is best to underwrite only the word wall or high-frequency words in the first half of the school year and then progress to all or most misspellings and omitted words in the second half of the school year. If you find a lot more than three or four misspellings, you may choose to circle the fourth, fifth, or other errors to indicate they are also incorrect, but not phonics flex them because you are focusing their attention on only those three or four words in that writing piece. In the next piece, you choose other errors.

2. Newcomer's Learning Targets – I encourage you to keep a simple log or record of what each Newcomer produces in their earlier writing; therefore, you can choose to focus on words with certain phoneme-grapheme or sound-letter correlation. For example, a Newcomer may write "f" instead of "th" in words like "fing" for "thing", "fis" for "this", and "fik" for "thick". You will underwrite the correct sound-letter relationship. After teacher underwriting a written piece, record this approximation on your checklist of sounds and letter production to plan targeted mini lessons.

3. Space on the Page – If not enough room on the original page, I observed some teachers performing underwriting of all the words on another paper if the Newcomer's writing piece is tight on the page. If you choose to write on another paper, adhere to that page over the original text with tape under the student's drawing so the original writing can be seen for grading purposes. Figures 7.3 to 7.5 are examples of TU with and without enough room to give you an idea of the variety of writing samples you may encounter depending on the student's age and the writing task assigned.

Editing for non-Newcomers during the writing process is often about self-review or peer review of grammatical forms and spelling errors. This requires a good peer level of English to complete such tasks. Editing for Newcomers who have such limited knowledge of English words and patterns is difficult at best. These ELs benefit more from a buildup of English than tasks asking them to point out errors. Therefore, teaching Newcomers words a letter sound at a time, called phonics flexing, uniquely boosts Newcomer's acquisition of English language patterns using their own words as written material. Over time your Newcomers will internalize

English orthographic mapping and sound-letter patterns, toward word-level reading and spelling (Betgevergiz, 2020) through explicit instruction and personalize literacy feedback which is why and how the specialized EL technique of PF was designed.

Looking at the samples below, it is clear that M.S. still struggles with English phonics and phonemic awareness, especially when it pertains to hearing and writing short and long vowel sounds and writing in proper English grammar and sentence structure.

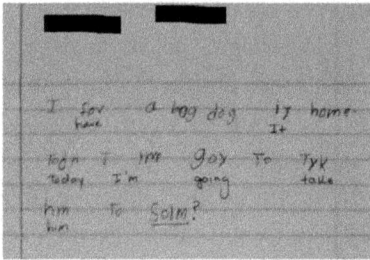

Left Figure 1.1: M.S.'s first sentence dictation, with "have" spelled as "fov."
Right Figure 1.2: M.S.'s final sentence dictation, with "have" spelled as "fus."

Figure 7.3 Teacher underwriting example with space to write

Source: Photo of the teacher model of teacher underwriting by Eugenia Krimmel during Millersville University's ESL Clinical Practicum, 2022.

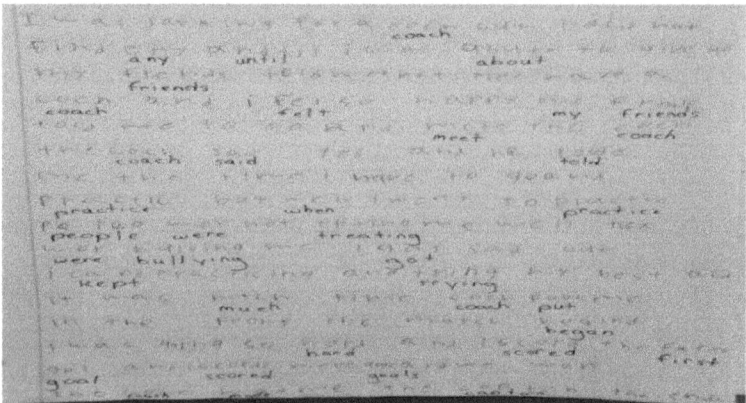

Figure 7.4 High school example of teacher underwriting

Source: Photo by Eugenia Krimmel during Millersville University's ESL Clinical Practicum, 2022.

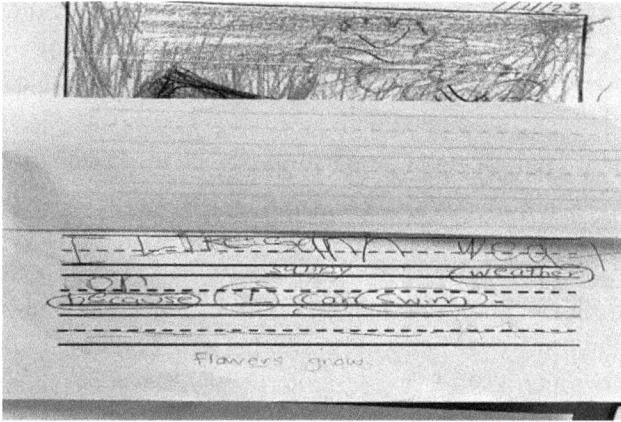

Figure 7.5 Attaching teacher underwriting over the original writing

Source: Photo by Eugenia Krimmel during Millersville University's
ESL Clinical Practicum, 2022.

EL-Integrated Technique # 6 – Phonics Flexing

What Is Phonics Flexing?

According to literacy education researcher Kristina Robertson, in an article on the Colorin' Colorado website (www.colorincolorado.org) (n.d.), it is best to teach phonics in context, especially for older students including ELs. Robertson goes on to state the use of authentic text is best for teaching phonics and reading comprehension. Teachers can call attention to keywords' sound-letter correlation in context as a means of consciousness-raising of both phonics and meaning for more effective and accelerated language acquisition. She also highlights the fact that students' writing itself is authentic text (Robertson, n.d.) and is age-appropriate for older ELs who typically find phonics instructional materials made for younger learners. Older ELs do not connect with those childish materials. The EL Writing Process centers on the use of ELs' experiences written in as much English as they can. TU fills in the linguistic gaps of their written text while phonics is taught by flexing across incorrect words helping ELs hear and see the correct words in English.

The EL technique of PF occurs during guided, personalized feedback time in quick individualized editing conferences in which the teacher models the sound-letter correspondence and the English word patterns from what Newcomers wrote. With this kind of feedback over several months, Newcomers will acquire language patterns and will gain confidence in their English writing skills.

Unlike PF, "sounding out" is a text-to-speech technique used mainly during reading instruction. Because Newcomers have another language system in their heads, asking them if something "sounds right" is useless. It is all English to them, so it all sounds correct in the beginning until they gain an intermediate level of proficiency and can distinguish English words better. ELs who become good at sounding out English are often called "word callers" because they "cracked the code"; however, most early "word callers" have little to no comprehension of what they are reading aloud. Decoding does not ensure comprehension.

PF, on the other hand, is a speech-to-text technique best used during the guided feedback of TU. The PF technique starts with spoken words during the read-back activity by the Newcomer pronouncing what they intended to write. Teachers slow down their speech and emphasize sounds and words to allow Newcomer authors time to distinguish phonemes within their own words and phrases while teachers point out or write the letters. Hence, PF is more of a speech-to-text activity by connecting the oral language and discussion of the images to written English-patterned words or phrases. Newcomers usually only hear rapid English speech in conversation; therefore, slowing down the oral language while looking at the written letters and words gives Newcomers time to make connections and internalize the patterns.

Do not merely correct the Newcomer's writing. PF uses positive reinforcement to achieve conscientiousness raising and attention to correct letter-sound relations for the bilingual brain to retain the patterns. Point out the correct sound-to-letter correspondence your Newcomer produced by tapping those letters. Ignore any incorrectly written letters as you proceed through the PF technique by not tapping or pointing it out. The positive reinforcement of these personalized phonics lessons gives Newcomers a unique opportunity to learn using their own English writing trials and triumphs.

Avoid these useless and deficit-model phrases when phonics flexing with Newcomers:

1. Do you understand? Newcomers will usually say "yes" just to please you or to only acknowledge they heard you. Even if they repeat what they are supposed to do, that does not ensure they know "how" to do the task. Show them, don't tell them what actions they need to take.
2. Does that sound right? To Newcomers it is all English, so everything sounds right. This is a useless question until they reach more advanced stages of language proficiency. Have them repeat a word or phrase they just tackled as a means of helping them move that utterance from short-term to long-term memory.
3. "You forgot the letter __". This is the worst sentence to say to a Newcomer. When Newcomers omit letters in a word, it is not because they *forget* it but rather because it is not *internalized* enough in their head. Saying they forgot something indicates a failure on their part. PF is designed to build Newcomers' spelling skills without deficit-based comments that defeat their efforts.

What Does Phonics Flexing Look Like?

When you come upon a misspelled or missing word during the TU process, begin the PF process with an assets-based mindset. In other words, be sure to praise what Newcomers have produced correctly and simply add the corrections as a matter of fact. Some teachers say degrading comments like, "You forgot your 'a' in 'npkin'" or "You dropped your second 'b' in 'rabit'". These types of comments are also deficit-based and have no place in teaching any students, especially Newcomer ELs. ELs do not necessarily have these sounds, letters, or English patterns in their heads, so how could they "forget" or "drop" letters when writing? This type of interaction can lead any writer to doubt themselves, and it will lower confidence in their own abilities. Praise the triumphs during PF through tapping correct letters for positive reinforcement and ignore or do not tap any incorrect letters or words during PF. In fact, you can apply this simple practice anytime you are addressing ELs' written production in English.

Phonics Flexing Process

When you encounter a misspelled word during the TU process, proceed through this whole-part-whole protocol:

1.	Pronounce the whole word they attempted to write.
2.	Tap any correct letters they produced in that word as you begin to highlight one phoneme at a time – part of the word. Praise the Newcomers if they wrote the correct letter within the word they wanted to write as you point or tap it. "Good you heard the /sound/ and wrote the /letter/"; that is all you have to say.
3.	Pronounce the phoneme as you write the correct letter (s) below their writing and flex through by saying the whole word.
4.	Repeat these steps for the next phoneme of the word. Again, if your Newcomer wrote the correct letter, tap, and praise, if no letter or the incorrect letter, no tap. Simply write the letter (s) and pronounce the phoneme and then flex through by pronouncing the whole word again.
5.	Do not scratch out or alter student writing at all. Either put a dot under the word or draw a zigzag line to show them you are addressing that word. You will use their writing samples for diagnostic purposes and to show students and families their writing progress. Remember – mistakes teach us, so do not cross out. Model correct English writing below or next to their writing. You may have to use lines to connect your corrections to their original writing.

Phonics Flexing Example

The word "tapl" for "table" was written incorrectly by one of your Newcomers:

1. Say the whole correct English word first., "table". Then proceed to the first phoneme.
2. Tap the Newcomer's written letter /t/ while saying the sound /t/ and writing "t" under the word "tapl" or on another piece of paper and then flex across all the sounds by saying the complete word "table".
3. Next, tap the written "a" and blend the long /ā/ pronunciation with the /t/ to pronounce /tā/ as you write the "a" next to the "t" under the student's word and then flex across the word by saying the complete word "table".

4. Next, ignore the "p" and pronounce /b/ as you write the letter "b" in the word below the student's writing and say /tāb/ and then flex across the word by saying the complete word "table".

5. Next, tap the "L" and pronounce /L/ as you write the letter "l" in the word below to form /tabl/ and flex across the word by saying the complete word "table".

6. Lastly, add the silent "e" to the word and tell the student "table" has a silent "e" that they will learn about soon. Flex across the word one last time by saying the complete word "table".

Another way to look at the progression of PF for the word "tapl" is illustrated in Table 7.2.

In addition, this consciousness-raising technique gives Newcomers time to process the sound-letter correspondence in an authentic setting rather than a prescriptive reading lesson with less connection to their own written thoughts. During the PF activity, you can ask Newcomers to "watch your mouth" so they will focus on the oral pronunciation of English sounds that they attempted to write. This is a critical step for Newcomers in correlating phonics and spelling of English patterns one sound and letter at a time. Older Newcomers truly need this level of explicit foundational instruction that is not built into their academic program.

To help you visualize what TU with PF looks like on student writing, see Figure 7.6. Note the teacher provided cohesive sentence frames such as "I like . . .", "Another reason I like . . .", and "Most importantly . . .", so Newcomers can complete the sentences with their own thoughts.

Table 7.2 Phonics Flexing Example

Tapl
T -ā-b-l (silent -e)
Tā -b-l (silent -e)
Tāb -l (silent -e)
Tābl (silent -e)

Note the Newcomer has heard you pronounce this word "table" five times in the span of a few seconds while equating the written grapheme or letter to the respective phonemes as you flexed through the word. This powerful repetition for learning and personalized connection to the word makes the feedback more meaningful to any language learner. You have now *accelerated* your Newcomer's literacy skills in phonics, spelling, and writing through their own words. What an impact!

Phase 2 : Teacher Underwriting and Phonics Flexing

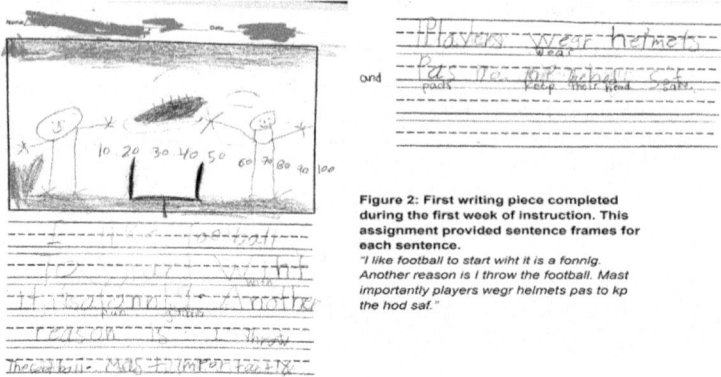

Figure 2: First writing piece completed
during the first week of instruction. This
assignment provided sentence frames for
each sentence.
"I like football to start wiht it is a fonnlg.
Another reason is I throw the football. Mast
importantly players wegr helmets pas to kp
the hod saf."

Figure 7.6 Student writing with phonics flexing

Source: Photo by Eugenia Krimmel during Millersville University's
ESL Clinical Practicum, 2022.

Sample 1

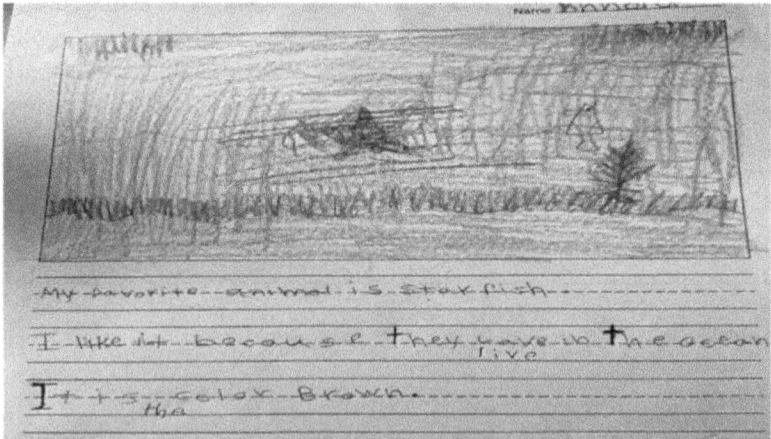

Figure 7.7 Minimum teacher underwriting and phonics flexing

Source: Photo by Eugenia Krimmel during Millersville University's
ESL Clinical Practicum, 2024.

As Newcomers become more confident and skilled English writers, TU and PF are needed less often. Figure 7.7 shows you a case of this stage in an EL's writing progression.

Phonological and Phonics Differences for Newcomer ELs

PF for Newcomers, as mentioned above, taps into different phonemes and sound-symbol correspondence compared to English. Start the PF activity by elongating or slow pronunciation of the target sounds in written words so Newcomers can distinguish those sounds better. You may be asking yourself the question most teachers ask: which letters, consonants, or vowels should I emphasize or teach first? My answer is simple – highlight the letters your Newcomer authors wrote while in the writing workshop. You may have to deliver mini lessons on some letter sounds like "x" and "z", but during the PF process you should be able to cover them all.

Expect some Newcomers to delay in producing certain consonants and vowels in speaking and writing because some phonemes may not exist in their native language. The most common example of a difficult phoneme-grapheme correlation is voiced and voiceless /th/ because few languages have this phoneme other than English. In some cultures, extending the tongue beyond the teeth is a rude gesture; therefore, to produce the voiced /th/ as in "think" is considered impolite. Many ELs use /t/, /s/, /z/, or /d/ when they encounter the /th/ in decoding or speaking English. For this reason, teaching Newcomers to hear and write /th/ takes a longer time than it does for most English speakers. Those who *do* have this phoneme in their language such as Castellaño Spanish speakers of Spain rarely struggle to produce /th/ in spoken English but may misspell it at first because their home language letters "z" and "c+i" produce that sound.

An English phonetic chart may help you awaken your inner linguist to recognize sound-spelling correspondence needed for effective TU and PF. One resource you may want to explore is the English Alphabetic Code website (https://phonicsinternational.com/unit1_pdfs/The%20English%20Alphabetic%20Code%20-%20complete%20picture%20chart.pdf) or the International Phonetic Alphabet for American

English (https://easypronunciation.com/en/american-english-pronunciation-ipa-chart). These resources will help you decode and encode English for your Newcomers as you study these to gain confidence in your own phonics teaching skills.

Cross-Linguistic Analysis (see Appendix G) is a study of similarities and differences between two languages to predict new language learners' transfer errors and struggles. For example, Arabic has no /p/ sound; therefore, "pencil" will often be written "bencil" by Arabic speakers. Time, attention to, and deliberate practice help Arabic-speaking students to not only write the /p/ sound as a "p" letter but also help Arabic speakers to distinguish between a /p/ and /b/ when speaking in English. If sounds do not exist in their language, the sound will be more difficult for Newcomers to grasp and recall orally and in writing.

Lado (1957) and Fries (1945) characterized first language (L1) transfer as the application of native language elements onto expressions or sentences in a second language. However, Schachter (1983, 1992) acknowledged the possibility of learners possessing incomplete proficiency in the second language and suggested that L1 transfer and delays in internalizing new sounds might be a result of a gap in language acquisition of the new language; therefore, the L1 sounds or letters are produced to fill the void. For example, when your Newcomer Arabic speakers write a "b" instead of a "p", it is most likely due to what is called translanguaging. They produce language from the repertoire in their heads. The letter "b" in this scenario is the closest approximation to "p"; therefore, by not knowing of a "p", the Newcomers go with what they know.

Whether you agree with research on L1 transfer and to what degree, I can assure you, as an experienced second language teacher for over 30 years to date, students do indeed struggle with sounds and letters unfamiliar to them. You are advised to know the characteristics of a Newcomer's first language to help you understand the possible reasons for errors. In my mind, it is an interesting study as well as a point of conversation with students as you ask them about their language. As they may not know how to answer all your questions about their language, you may have to search for information on your own.

The Cross-Linguistic Analysis Examples in Appendix A are meant to get you started on this language informational search. A fillable digital form of this resource is available in the Support Materials folder, so you can expand the chart when you learn about other languages your Newcomers bring to your classroom. Enjoy the discovery of new languages. Learn about language phonology, phonics, and writing systems through a digital search and/or from native speakers of those languages to complete the chart for those new language entries. Start your inquiry at www.omniglot.com or www.ethnologue.com.

EL Coach's Corner: Editing and Revising Step for Newcomers

Scaffolds are best used at the beginning of learning but must be pulled back as the learner develops the skill. The same is true of TU and PF are personalized instruction techniques involving error correction and foundational literacy instruction. Teachers who continually correct or point out errors for ELs even into their advanced levels do them a disservice by not allowing their language acquisition to deepen through self-correction. Errors and occasional mistakes are teaching tools that each brain needs to tackle in its own way in order to learn from them. When your Newcomers are at the entering stage, they need you to point out their errors. As they acquire more and more English proficiency, you must pull back on pointing out errors by requiring self-correction over time. This is the best practice for the bilingual brain to acquire a new language.

According to Sousa in his book *How the Brain Learns* (2010), learning occurs when the brain goes from a state of confusion to understanding. The learning process of language and/or concepts is far more complex than that simple phrase implies. At first, the bilingual Newcomer brain cannot even identify errors because it is so busy producing what it can of the new language. It is in total or almost total confusion. For this reason, the teacher points out errors and models corrections.

As the bilingual brain acquires more English proficiency and understands more, it can self-correct with support at first and eventually can self-correct on its own. Table 7.3 indicates the progression of error correction showing how to gradually guide ELs toward self-correction of their written and spoken English.

Table 7.3 Progression of Error Correction for ELD Writing Instruction

Level 1	Level 2	Level 3	Level 4
The teacher identifies errors and makes corrections by modeling proper patterns.	The teacher identifies errors and encourages ELs to self-correct; if ELs are not able, then the teacher makes corrections but encourages self-correction next time.	The teacher identifies errors for ELs but requires ELs to self-correct. The teacher checks for accuracy.	The teacher tells ELs there are errors in a sentence or paragraph. ELs must identify and correct errors. The teacher checks for accuracy.

Personalized instruction such as TU and PF customizes learning experiences to meet the unique needs of individual Newcomers acquiring English literacy. The EL-focused techniques integrated into your writing workshop protocol play a vital role in addressing diverse language backgrounds and proficiency levels by creating a more accessible and engaging learning environment. Your Newcomers will begin their language learning journey at their own pace and build a solid foundation for language acquisition and literacy skills.

Reflection Questions:

1. Explain why the TU protocol is adapted for different Newcomer writing situations. Describe those changes.
2. Describe how the Science of Reading principles are implemented through PF.
3. Practice PF of other common Newcomer spelling approximations. Circle the EL letters you would tap when using PF with a Newcomer who wrote the sentences shown in Figure 7.7

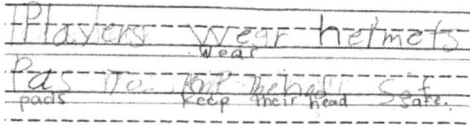

Figure 7.7A Sample 7A image

Source: Photo by Eugenia Krimmel during Millersville University's
ESL Clinical Practicum, 2022.

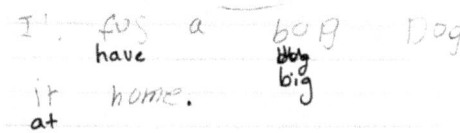

Figure 7.7B Sample 7B image

Source: Photo by Eugenia Krimmel during Millersville University's
ESL Clinical Practicum, 2023.

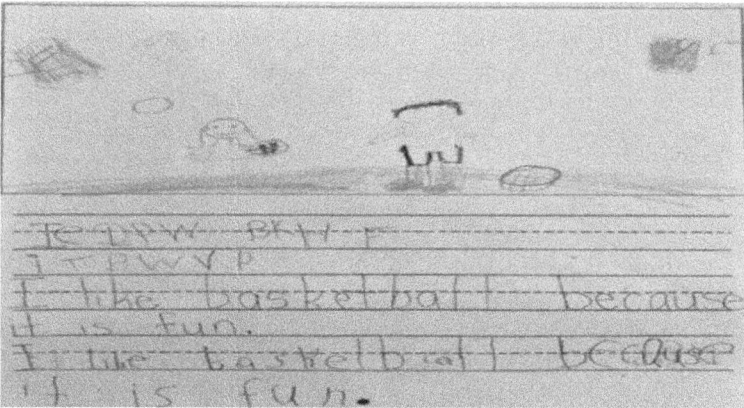

Figure 7.7C Sample 7C image

Source: Photo by Eugenia Krimmel during Millersville University's
ESL Clinical Practicum, 2024.

References

Betgevergiz, L. (2020). What is orthographic mapping? *Institute for Multi-sensory Education Journal*. https://journal.imse.com/orthographic-mapping/

Chang, C. Y. (2016). Two decades of research in L2 peer review. *Journal of Writing Research, 8*(1), 81–117. https://doi.org/10.17239/jowr-2016.08.01.03

Fries, C. C. (1945). *Teaching and learning English as a foreign language*. University of Michigan Press.

Lado, R. (1957). *Linguistics across cultures*. University of Michigan Press.

Ramirez, H., & Jones, D. (2013). Effects of reading strategies and the writing process with written recasts on second language achievement. *Administrative Issues Journal, 3*(1), Article 9.

Robertson, K. (n.d.). Phonics instruction for middle and high school ELLs. *Colorin Colorado*. https://www.colorincolorado.org/comment/reply/56601

Rutherford, W. E., & Sharwood Smith, M. (1985). Consciousness-raising and universal grammar. *Applied Linguistics, 6*, 274–282.

Schachter, J. (1983). A new account of language transfer. In S. Gass & L. Selinker (Eds.), *Language transfer in language learning* (pp. 98–111). Newbury House.

Schachter, J. (1992). A new account of language transfer. In S. Gass & L. Selinker (Eds.), *Language transfer in language learning* (pp. 32–46). John Benjamins.

Sousa, D. A. (2010). *How the ell brain learns*. Corwin Press.

Tanaka, K. (2010). The philosophical, political, and the practical dimensions of English for academic purposes education: A focus on critical thinking. *Meiji Gakuin Review International & Regional Studies, 37*, 67–77.

8 Publish Step

Overview of the Publish Step

The publishing step is a crucial milestone in the writing process, offering students a chance to showcase their creative efforts and unique thoughts. This final stage marks the completion of a writing project and underscores the significance of the entire writing journey. For all writers, the act of publishing goes beyond personal accomplishment; it cultivates a sense of pride and confidence in their abilities. Moreover, publishing provides a tangible audience for students' writing, whether it is their classmates, teachers, parents, or the broader school community. This final writing accomplishment and reader feedback not only validate students' efforts but may also inspire them to continue honing their writing skills.

Additionally, the publishing step fosters a sense of community within the writing workshop time, as students celebrate each other's achievements and offer support and encouragement. Ultimately, the publishing step in the EL Writing Process empowers Newcomers to see themselves as authors capable of creating meaningful and impactful writing in English that resonates with others. Through the process of refining their work for publication, Newcomers engage with new vocabulary, practice English language patterns, and express their unique perspectives in a new language.

EL WRITING PROCESS

Publish Step
- 7) Write to Spell Mini Lessons
- 8) Rewrite for Repetition & Publishing

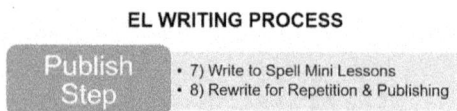

Image 8.a EL Writing Process publish step

EL-Integrated Technique # 7 – Write to Spell Mini Lessons

EL writing is a methodology, not a program or a book series. It is a methodology, not a fit-in-this-box type of writing protocol. No external company can know what your students need and how they need specialized instruction; therefore, you are encouraged to use the resources around you to teach mini lessons on foundational phonics, spelling, and writing, using Newcomers' own written work as authentic material. EL writing's flexibility in the use of materials, student-driven target goals, and varied lesson objectives sets it apart from more prescriptive methods of structured literacy for older Newcomers in particular.

Foundational literacy mini lessons can begin with small groups as Newcomers finish writing even if other students are still writing, or you can wait for whole group instruction. The EL Writing Process trained teachers employed a "status board" practice at the beginning of each writing session. Each student was to indicate which step they were on in the writing process once the draw-to-draft step started. Some teachers used a poster board for the whole class to mark which step they were at that day. Other teachers used laminated personalized cards, as shown in Table 8.1, for students to color the star, indicating which stage they were in that day.

You will know instantly which students are at what stage of the writing process and can group them by activity. When they have completed drawing or writing, they can color in the next star or move their name along the writing process status board from drawing to editing to rewriting as they progress through the writing workshop steps. After you complete TU and PF processes, Newcomers move their name plaque or color their cards to the rewriting for publishing step. If they finish with their final draft and others are still working, they have extension activities ready to keep

Table 8.1 Personalized Writing Step Status Card

☆	Draw-to-Draft Step
☆	Editing and Revision Step
☆	Rewriting for Publishing Step

them occupied. Remember to model this status board or card routinely for quite a few times.

This EL technique of designing mini lessons incorporates targeted errors from Newcomers' written pieces into planned literacy instruction for a small group or the whole class. Some Newcomer misspellings may be common among other students as well but for a different reason. Other emerging errors result from first language interference or the newness of English patterns not yet internalized; therefore, your Newcomers may have misspellings and omitted words purely because of the new language learning process.

For example, several Newcomers may drop the "n" in "nd" words like "friend or find". That point will be your mini lesson's target goal within that cycle. Another issue that may appear in Newcomers' early writing is incorrect vowel sounds, such as writing an "i" for the long /e/ sound as in "ich" for "each" and "grin" for "green". Your mini lessons will be specific and targeted to make the most impact on the brain. Show them one correction at a time, giving their minds time to absorb and correct one thing at a time.

Literacy mini lessons bring English rules and norms to light for ELs to acquire when their bilingual brains are ready to move the item from short-term to working memory. Like the teachable moments in the personalized error correction of PF during the TU process, literacy mini lessons highlight just one or two linguistic points that Newcomers' brains need to pay attention to and internalize.

Focused Mini Lessons for Newcomers

What are the target goals of EL Writing Process mini lessons? There is no scope and sequence nor a planned progression of linguistic points. This technique is responsive to student errors. You are encouraged to have a proactive sequence of phonics, spelling, and writing instructional points for your whole class according to your curriculum. EL writing, however, is designed as timely and reactive to beginner errors with targeted instruction. Based on Newcomers' writing, drawings, or labeled images, conduct mini lessons at the letter, word, and sentence levels as appropriate to the errors that emerge. Using Newcomer's own writing to model corrections at this point serves as the instructional level material for Newcomers to move along the continuum of writing skill development. I suggest you keep a running list of the misspellings and errors you see from Newcomers in any given writing workshop based on the TU and PF activities. These linguistic points become the lesson objectives. Over time you will see a pattern.

How Mini Is an EL Writing Mini Lesson?

Teachers should take a mini lesson no longer than 10 to 15 minutes a day. That is how a targeted mini lesson must be. The time spent doing the "show, not tell" activities of literacy mini lessons will consist of a target skill, model or mentor text, immediate practice, and quick reinforcing feedback. Making these "digestible bites" of skill development a routine within the writing process allows Newcomers to take in the small pieces of English patterns that build upon each other.

Planning a foundational literacy mini lesson is crucial because you can so easily turn a mini into a maxi! The EL writing mini lesson template, shown in Table 8.2, approaches planning by working backward from goal to measure of learning. Choose the mini lesson's learning target or lesson objectives and then start building your plan by recording how you will

Table 8.2 Mini Lesson Template

Learning Target/ Lesson Objective	Measuring Learning	Practice Activity Procedure	Materials Needed (for presenting, practicing, and measuring)
Objective (s)	Number Correct or Rubric	Hook & Instructional Activities	Visuals, handouts, videos, props, rubric, etc.

Table 8.3 Mini Lesson Completed Example

Learning Objective	Measuring Learning	Practice Activity Procedure	Materials Needed (for presenting, practicing, and measuring)
Recognize word family -ink -ick because my Newcomers mix these spellings	Number correct identifying rhyming pairs	1. With picture cards, show STs 4–5 words in each family: -"ick" and –"ink" 2. Minimal pairs to identify rhyming pairs with short "i" ending in "k" -ick and -ink; example "sink" for "sick" and "pink" for "pick"	Present rhyming words in English Practice paper numbered 1–5 T. gives 5 pairs like: sick-pick, sink-tick, link-lick, etc.

present the concept. Once decided, plan the practice activity, what text you will use to model the target goal, and what materials are required (e.g. handouts, EL writing sample, sticky notes, index cards, and foldables). Lastly, write out the measure of learning of this linguistic point.

This planner is short to reflect how mini the lesson should be. Table 8.3 gives you an idea of how to complete the foundational literacy mini lesson planner, but of course, you should use whatever format your brain prefers. Keep a record, though, do not just "wing it" because you want to know what you have covered within the quarter or school year. I highly recommend checking off your mini lesson objectives on your English Language

Arts curriculum as a means of showing that these linguistic points have been presented.

This exact activity (shown in Table 8.3) was conducted by one of the teacher trainees in the practicum course program. One Newcomer said the pair "sick–pick" did not rhyme because the first sounds were different, but "link-lick" rhymed because of the first sounds. Despite the teacher explaining and modeling rhyming words previously, the Newcomer did not understand the concept. Many Newcomers fail to recognize rhyming words in beginning English stages, but it is unclear why because other languages surely have rhyming words. Nonetheless, scheduling mini lessons on rhyming words should be a routine part of your word family or decoding instruction.

Linking Newcomers' writing needs to the mini lesson objectives directly addresses their current struggles with foundational English literacy skills. Another common focus of your mini lessons will be distinguishing and spelling high-frequency words. When learning a new language, all words run together in a sentence until one can distinctly hear a single word from another word. PF during the guided feedback time draws attention to single phonemes and words enhancing Newcomer ability to distinguish sounds within words and words within sentences. Mini lessons reinforce those distinctions if you isolate morphological endings like the three ways to pronounce final -ed or final -s/es/ies.

For older beginner Newcomers, mini lesson objectives may be beyond English letter formation if their first language also uses the Latin alphabet like English. However, if their written language uses Arabic, Chinese, or Cyrillic scripts, for example, these Newcomers will need to learn letter formation and written word directionality. Otherwise, mini lessons will center on sound-symbol correlations and omitted words. ELs of all language backgrounds struggle with "dropping" words not used in their first language such as the verb "to be" and articles like "a/an" and "the". In addition, prepositions confuse most non-native English speakers despite hearing them, so they do not write these in the beginning stages.

Hand and finger spelling clues or gestures to help Newcomers distinguish sounds and syllables in a word can accelerate English skill development. Be aware, however, that hand gestures are not all universal. In particular, the thumbs up and okay signs in English hold different meanings among world cultures. If you get a surprised or negative reaction from a

Newcomer, simply explain what meaning the gesture has in America and why you are using that gesture in your teaching practice. They will come to understand the significance and will take in the new meaning. You may want to simply ask if it means something different in their culture, but do not ask for details. The response may be inappropriate for the classroom.

Should Mini Lessons Focus on Standard American English or My Dialect?

According to linguists William Kretzschmar and Charles Meyer (2012), the term *Standard American English* customarily refers to a variation of the English language that is generally used in [oral and written] professional communication in the United States and taught in American schools. English is a global language with many versions and dialects; however, there are conventional patterns, rules, and uses English speakers of a particular English version understand. This is what is meant by "standard" and can vary from place to place even within the United States. I recommend you teach the English dialect in the area where you teach. Differences between vowel sounds from the southern states and northern states may arise, for example, but you will teach pronunciation and decoding of whichever state or region you are in at the time. Newcomers will pick up the local accent and pronunciation of classmates and those around them as they acquire the language.

Mini Lessons for Vocabulary Building

Your goal for Newcomers as with all students is reading comprehension when planning your writing instruction, right? To that end, your mini lessons for Level 1 Newcomers should include an explicit focus on meaning and use of words they wrote or new words within a text. Best practices for teaching Newcomers vocabulary and word choice fall into three categories: visual, linguistic, and movement.

Visual (use of images, icons, and images)

- Picture-word matches can be tricky at times if Newcomers' backgrounds have a different or no point of reference

- Word walls with pictures is good for Newcomers to process by having it available during class time to take in one word and image at a time.
- Labeling images with Tier 1 (everyday words), Tier 2 (general academic words), and Tier 3 keywords for the lesson; great for distinguishing words from others within a context.
- Vocabulary board games or card games in person and online

Linguistic (use of other words to explain the meaning of use of an English word)

- Use true cognates (words that have the same sound and meaning in both languages) when possible; you can look up some keywords to see if they have a cognate from English to the Newcomer's language. True cognates serve as a point of reference; however, some can be false cognates. Those are words that have a similar sound but different meanings. Be aware of these, too, if you can.
- Synonym strings (link synonyms together in degrees of connotation and model what you can. For example, the student knows: talk (v). Put in a string of words from loud talk to soft talk and demonstrate each (scream, yell, talk, state, whisper, and murmur)

Movement (use of the body to teach meaning and use)

- Total Physical Response (TPR) movement activities like gestures and acting out using the sequence of "I do, We do, You do" with a short list of words or phrases. Introduce and model, repeat as a group, then the teacher calls out the words or phrases in a random order to see how well Newcomers remembered the word and matched the meaning. Great repetition for moving words to working memory.
- Vocab Improvement – a round-robin activity in which ELs each get a separate word; they say the word and act it out, and the next EL says the previous word or words and then says their word while acting it out. The last student has to say and act them all out. Excellent repetition in a peer-teaching setting.
- Show, Draw, and Make Faces – This is a strategy I witnessed at a general education literacy conference and adapted it to Level 1 Newcomers. Choose a storybook with pictures that is not too long or

too short. Even older students like the occasional children's picture book. Beforehand, read the book to pick out five to ten vocabulary words depending on the age of the students. These are the words you want to highlight for contextual meaning. Give each student a blank paper or whiteboard. Of the ten words you chose from the book, decide which Newcomers can "show" by acting out, which can be drawn quickly, and which can be best shown through facial expressions.

For example, read *The Snails Wonder Journey* by Aruna Keerthi Gamage (2024).
In this story you can highlight these words:

Show me (actions) – laugh, floating, crawls
Draw – snail, feet, mountains, and bus
Make Faces – sad, happily/happy, think to yourself

Have all students participate so your Newcomers can learn new words. Some students will think it is silly, but there may be native English speakers who have not truly thought about these words so intently. A teacher in one of my ESL teaching clinical courses emailed me after trying Show, Draw, and Make Faces to let me know how her Newcomers were very engaged and looked to other students for meaning and understanding while her native English speakers thought it was just a fun time activity. She realized how important targeted Level 1 strategies can be for Newcomers. If you find this too basic for the majority of your class, reserve it for small-group instruction with only Newcomers.

EL-Integrated Technique # 8 – Rewrite for Repetition and Publishing

Although rewriting is simply copying the TU version, this action has a benefit for Newcomers. Repetition, according to David Sousa, author of *How the ELL Brain Learns* (2010), is one pathway to commit sensory input from short-term to working to long-term memory. By rewriting the corrected TU version of their own thoughts, Newcomers practice familiar and newly corrected spelling and grammatical patterns by copying their own words themselves.

As you well know, simply internalizing phonics and spelling rules does not lead to comprehension. The EL writing technique of rewriting involves Newcomers *copying with comprehension* which combines writing words Newcomers know mostly from their own thoughts or a very recent class discussion. It is at this beginning acquisition stage that celebrating any production of English is a triumph. Modeling correct patterns, also known as "recasting", is one of the most effective research-based strategies for error correction at the beginning stages of language acquisition (Dilans, 2010).

For some Newcomer brains, rewriting is effective for organizing thoughts and seeing patterns; however, not all minds work that way. Another research-based error correction strategy for higher beginners is giving feedback prompts for self-correcting errors (Lyster, 2004). When the corrected text process is completed, you should read back the text to the Newcomer writer while pointing at each word to reinforce the one-to-one relationship. Other students are encouraged to join the choral read if this is done in a small group setting.

Note that initially when Newcomers rewriting their work with teacher's underwriting corrections, the reading level of that newly created text can be above the Newcomer's current reading level due to added or translated-into-English words. As a result, students may struggle to independently read back their writing and will require practice in the form of choral reading with you. For Newcomers, this choral reading activity helps them learn more English letters, words, and phrases because the text is as authentic as their own thoughts. This in turn contributes to their brain's ability to grasp the word patterns. For now, you just want to celebrate what they produced in written English whether just a letter, word, phrase, or sentence. Their writing shows what they internalized.

Newcomers' published rewritten pieces should be shared with class-mates in small groups or posted on the walls of the classrooms. An audience gives writing a purpose. Figure 8.1 shows the final draft rewritten by the Newcomer on another page, whereas Figure 8.2 shows the final draft rewritten by the Newcomer on a separate page that was taped over the original. Both ways of rewriting to final draft for publishing are accept-able. You can make that determination based on the class situation or goal

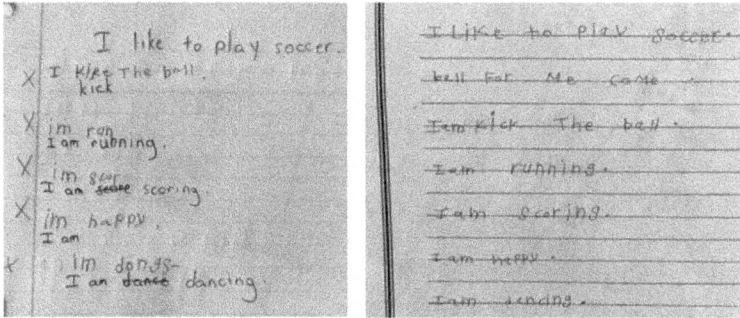

Figure 8.1 Newcomer writing sample from TU to the final draft

Source: Photo of published or finalized student writing by Eugenia Krimmel during Millersville University's ESL Clinical Practicum, 2023.

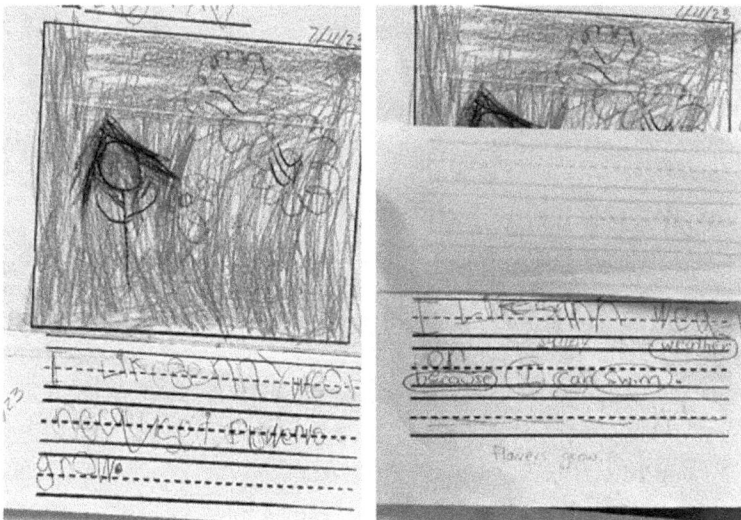

Figure 8.2 Teacher underwriting to the final published version

Source: Photo of published student work taped over original writing by Eugenia Krimmel during Millersville University's ESL Clinical Practicum, 2023.

of publishing such as creating a class library of student works or sharing at an Author's Chair event with families. Most often I imagine your writing workshop goals center on developing your students' skills of writing in an assessment-type portfolio in print or digitally.

Publishing Options

To show student writing in the moment and over time, a writing assessment portfolio or e-portfolio is a great option. What form will that be in? Paper booklets or digital versions can be created through PowerPoint, Nearpod, Book Creator, Google Keep, or part of a Microsoft Class Notebook, among other digital platforms. Before sharing Newcomers' writing for peer editing or simply a read-aloud, check with them about sharing their writing. Some Newcomers, like their peers, love that spotlight and others are terrified of the attention. It is best to ask for volunteers only if sharing in front of an audience.

By publishing these stories and booklets in a class library with the author's permission, of course, Newcomers can eventually find something to read in English at their instructional or independent level. Newcomers benefit from reading TU-corrected peer-created English text as they internalize English sound, word, and sentence patterns, so include the first and final drafts together when publishing. This is especially true for older Newcomers, for whom lower-level reading materials are geared toward younger readers.

Coach's Corner: Publish Step for Newcomers

1. Teaching High-Frequency Words for Writing Fluency

Your goal in teaching both ELs and non-ELs is to help them reach automaticity of reading and writing words by knowing word form, meaning, and use. To that end, you can also assess your Newcomers' sight word knowledge baseline. Newcomers may have learned some print environmental words before arriving in your classroom. To measure their recognition of sight words, periodically assess high-frequency word recognition through district testing or your own checklist.

By testing words in isolation, ELs do not have a context in which to guess the word. If you are not sure which sight words to assess, you could follow this list of progressively more sight words: The High-Frequency Words Assessment List available at

https://drive.google.com/file/d/1iJA6ysr6vgAuc_88aMg72Br RqbJ1EnpK/view.

Mini Lessons on Sight and High-Frequency Words

High-frequency words appear in texts and environmental print. The repetition of seeing these words, hopefully in context, contributes to Newcomers' new language acquisition. These common words can be either phonetically regular or irregular according to the rules of English spelling and decoding. Sight words, also known as heart words, usually do not follow phonetic rules; therefore, these words must be memorized by sight or learned by heart to recall quickly. You are advised to highlight both high-frequency and sight/heart words in your foundational literacy mini lessons as these appear in your Newcomers' written pieces.

For Newcomers, the common practice of sending home word lists to memorize is particularly ineffective, as it often fails to support their unique learning needs (Farrell et al., 2013). Instead, integrating high-frequency word instruction into interactive phonics lessons provides a more effective approach. New language learners require contextualized and meaningful learning opportunities for language development because just being exposed to these words without comprehension is equally ineffective.

They need comprehension and phonetic instruction. As they spend more time in your class, the more Newcomers will learn spelling and phonics knowledge. Most sight words do have some parts that follow the phonics rules and have parts that do not. Mini lessons should point out the regular parts and rulebreaker parts. Best practices for your mini lessons include repetition practice, storytelling, and word games like Heart Word Bingo, Heart Word Hunts, and group reading activities so that Newcomers learn decoding from peers.

2. Use of Translation Decreases

Our brains go to what is more comfortable. As you know, we think in our inner speech, but as proficiency increases in a new language, bilingual brains now have more to recall as needed. In week two of my ESL teaching practicum program, a Newcomer used a translation app to tell his teacher that "every day is getting easier [in English]". In week four, this

Newcomer wrote several pieces in English only without using a transla-tor. Every Newcomer varies in that timing, but most will get to that point of thinking in English within the first year. All the techniques in the EL Writing Process aim to accelerate Newcomers' basic literacy skills toward academic English success.

3. Author's Chair Activity

Newcomers may come from collectivist societies that are not comfortable being singled out for praise. I recommend teachers use more group praise practices to celebrate Newcomers' published writing after the Author's Chair-type activities. A quick group cheer should be proper praise. Types of cheers can include:

1. Countdown to Blast Off
2. Disco or Jazz Hands
3. Rollercoaster Arms
4. Cowboy Cheer complete with throwing a lasso action!

Reflection Questions:

1. What are the benefits of knowing the methodology of integrating the EL Writing Process versus using a prescriptive writing instruction program?
2. Do you know where the learning objectives of your foundational liter-acy mini lessons come from and why are those important?
3. Describe the backward planning approach to designing foundational literacy mini lessons for Newcomers. Why is it important to record your scope and sequence of mini lesson objectives throughout the school year?
4. Some writing instruction methods or programs do not encourage rewriting for publishing student work. Why is it a beneficial step for Newcomers?
5. What's the difference between sight words and high-frequency words? Describe effective strategies to integrate the teaching of both to Newcomers.

References

Dilans, G. (2010). Corrective feedback and l2 vocabulary development: Prompts and recasts in the adult esl classroom. *Canadian Modern Language Review/La Revue canadienne des langues vivantes, 66*(6), 787–816.

Farrell, L., Osenga, T., & Hunter, M. (2013). *A new model for teaching high frequency words*. Readsters. https://www.readsters.com/wp-content/uploads/2013/03/NewModelForTeachingHFWords.pdf

Gamage, A. K. (2024). *The snails wonder journey*. Cheapest Books Publishing.

Kretzschmar, W. A., Jr., & Meyer, C. F. (2012). The idea of standard American English. In *Standards of English: Codified varieties around the world*. Cambridge University Press.

Lyster, R. (2004). Differential effects of prompts and recasts in form-focused instruction. *Studies in Second Language Acquisition, 26*, 399.

Sousa, D. A. (2010). *How the ell brain learns*. Corwin Press.

The Final Word

9 Lessons Learned and Future Directions

You picked up this book wondering if the bilingual brain is different from the monolingual brain when it comes to learning English literacy, right? You had an idea that something was different, but you were not really sure what that difference truly was. Essentially all brains are built the same but what each hold is individualized. In the case of Newcomers and ELs in general, what is in their brains is another complex language system of sounds and patterns that hold meaning and thought. That is the reason we have to approach the teaching of writing and all subjects with intentional best practices, so we give Newcomers access to the curriculum.

This is why I wrote this book for educators like you. All ELs are general education students first and foremost; however, they have that other language in their heads that may interrupt their English and content learning for a while. To help them and you navigate this complex situation, I designed the EL Writing Process to integrate EL techniques into your writing instruction routine that are similar yet intentionally geared for Newcomers' success. Table 9.1 illustrates what the EL Writing Process is and is not for your planning, delivery, and assessment purposes.

As Hammond (2025) stated so aptly during a webinar that "we don't learn to read while reading; the act of reading is practice. We learn to read while talking, moving, and seeing".

The same holds true for Newcomers and writing. They do not learn writing only by writing because they must first learn through "comprehensible"

DOI: 10.4324/9781003610595-12

Table 9.1 What the EL Writing Process Is and Is Not

What the EL Writing Process Is . . .	What the EL Writing Process Is Not . . .
• a roadmap for teaching phonics, spelling, and writing to newcomer ELs of any age • a systematic protocol to achieve personalized error correction effectively • a method giving teachers confidence in their ability to provide impactful strategies • a method aimed at preventing reading & writing failure of ELs • standards-based literacy support	• one-size-fits-all • a prescriptive GPS-type program that gives you every detail so that you cannot tailor it to your newcomers' needs • a method supporting just one reading program • a separate protocol that can only be done in ESL-designated instruction but can be incorporated into English language arts literacy instruction • a replacement for your school's writing program

conversation, gestures, and visuals of all sorts. However, Hammond (2025) reminds us that humans are not designed for literacy. We must be taught the code of an oral language. Unless we know the code, reading looks like simple scribbles on paper. Coincidently, that is exactly how Newcomers see English in the early stages.

Newcomers of any age are often expected to run with comprehension before they can even take a step in making sense of the graphic symbols of English. The design of the EL Writing Process is to afford Newcomers the time and place to take those steps when practicing English writing after listening, moving, seeing, and comprehending. It may take them a while longer and a bit more practice to reach the peer level, but they will not start off well, and the gaps will grow without this systematic approach to teaching and learning English literacy.

Teaching with EL-Integrated Techniques

As you wrap your head around the EL Writing Process protocol and techniques, keep this "simple view of EL Writing" in mind:

EL Writing Process at a Glance

Pre-Writing Step

Setting up the background knowledge for Newcomers to comprehend more is crucial for their academic language acquisition, English literacy confidence, and retrieval practice. This is the first important step to any literacy learning through writing. Comprehension! What is the topic? What are the details of this topic?

For example, if your content topic is information about pollution, you want all your students to think about:

What it is.
How it is formed or created and who makes it.
What it looks like and where it is located.
Where it is found.
When did it start and why?

All these aspects of your topic "pollution" can be presented through seeing, moving, and organizing. Newcomers will not understand all the details, but they will get the gist of the topic and some key words through well-planned instruction for the whole class. Every student will benefit from critical thinking activities (shown in Table 9.2) geared to teaching Newcomers during the pre-writing stage.

Do Not Pre-Teach Vocabulary!

Shocking statement, I know, but think about it. Pre-teaching vocabulary words is disconnected, dull, and, for Newcomers, a disservice. Giving a list of words and having them fill out a Frayer model-type organizer seems random and not connected to anything before written content is presented. Truthfully, there is not much more mundane in one's school day than completing those dull vocabulary-definition lists of words that seem disconnected from one word to the next. For Newcomers, most English words are not connected to many other English words at this stage, so giving them lists of words and definitions is meaningless and ineffective. Use your classroom time more wisely. How?

Table 9.2 Pre-Writing Activities to Improve Critical Thinking

Listening	Seeing	Moving
Videos Peer academic conversations Teacher instructions Read aloud with images Information gap activities	Gestures Acting out Images with labels Books Venn diagrams Infographics T-charts Lists of related things Mapping	Manipulatives Language games Roleplay Index card and digital games Show, Draw, and Make Faces

The alternative is to pull vocabulary from the text, video, and/or images as you present the topic information. When you highlight a word after the video or mentor text, it now has a connected, comprehensible context. For each word you highlight, be sure to review it completely – not just the meaning. Take a few seconds to "break the code" of each vocabulary word. Sound it out by syllables, long or short vowel sounds, and any rule-breaking pronunciation. Doing so provides foundational literacy instruction for struggling readers and Newcomers alike. The phonics, decoding, and spelling rules you learned to help with PF can now be used in pre-writing when you highlight key vocabulary words. It takes just seconds, but this strategy is truly an effective service for your Newcomers, especially older ELs who have no phonics in their grade-level curriculum.

While Newcomers make sense of the detailed information and words of a topic, they also need to know what the final writing project should look like and how they will achieve it. This is where the task stays the same, compare-contrast, opinion, or narrative, etc., but the means to producing the writing task must be flexibly modified.

Show that the class is required to produce a story or an opinion piece, for example. In small groups or individually, you can show Newcomers how they will complete that assignment. For example, if the class is to write a three-part narrative with a beginning, middle, and end, provide Newcomers with a graphic organizer with three boxes for drawing, labeling, and completing a sentence frame. Show Newcomers a final model of their task. Then, demonstrate how to transfer their completed sentences into a story by rewriting their completed sentences in a paragraph or story form to publish. The other students can also use drawings, but they need not have sentence starters and can go right into story writing from their drawings or can draw after writing.

Newcomers have been introduced to words in this pre-writing stage. As the writing workshop continues, they will have to recall or retrieve English words and patterns through writing practice. TU and PF later in the process serve another crucial part of acquisition, but first, Newcomers must produce letters, words, or phrases.

Draw-to-Draft Writing Step

Being a secondary teacher and coaching ESOL teachers of all grade levels has allowed me to see and hear how Newcomers approach English writing tasks. Some Newcomers do nothing and think it will all just go away, while others attempt a bit of writing and then lose energy. When I suggest the additional writing step of draw-to-draft, the ESOL teachers often say they never thought of that. Sometimes, teachers tell me they do not have enough time, but I promised them it would make a difference – and it did.

Drawing is that one cognitive step between thinking of something to say or write and putting the thoughts out there "on paper". Newcomers have so little English that producing it without an interim step seems to stop them in their tracks. The images they see or draw trigger the retrieval of words, even from their first language and the new language they recently saw or heard in their class or elsewhere. Drawing is a comforting step forward instead of the big leap from their inner speech thoughts to a few sounds or words in English to putting those words on paper properly. Think about that – it is a giant mental leap.

Using the Word Line tool has proven equally effective at keeping Newcomers on task and writing continuously, as it shows them that using a placeholder is perfectly acceptable. Their reactions to using the Word Line tool seemed to indicate a sense of freedom and flow. They do not have to stop and look up a word. Newcomers just keep on writing what they can and seem to enjoy the brief conversations about those words during the TU process.

Draw-to-draft is a necessary step Newcomers need to move forward and not be stuck in the mental mud of fear and uncertainty of English reading and writing.

Edit and Revise Steps

This is the most unique step in the EL Writing Process. It is also the main difference between the general education and EL Writing Process. When I discovered the Orton-Gillingham (O-G) approach to teaching reading to dyslexics like my son, I knew instantly that the technique was valuable to all ELs, especially those new to the language. The O-G approach is the underpinning of most reading programs today, such as Wilson and Reading Horizons, among others.

Orton-Gillingham is a step-by-step learning process involving the rules and rulebreakers of sound-letter patterns in English that helps dyslexics build manageable executive functioning skills of reading.

(Orton-Gillingham.com, n.d.)

My practice of error correction improved using the O-G inspired method of personalization because I knew the phonics rules to better explain to Newcomers how their errors can be corrected in English. Before I learned the O-G approach, I literally said, "That is just the way we say it". I cringe thinking back on those times and how unhelpful that line truly was and is. Newcomers need pattern, rules, and focused repetition to master long and short vowels, our crazy consonants, and countless exceptions. That is the reason I designed the PF as I did know what Newcomers need to acquire English through explicit instruction and not just haphazardly catching what they can in class.

After the introduction of a word, recognition is key. TU and PF narrow Newcomers' attention to just one letter-sound relationship for a split second and then connect it to the whole word. Think about this – we assign writing to Newcomers who do not have the letter agility in their heads yet. We are asking them to run before even taking steps. That crucial stage of stepping one letter-sound and one word at a time proved to be powerful for so many Newcomers I observed in my clinics and classes. If your writing workshop time is running short, make the time and do not miss the indispensable technique of PF.

Publish Step

Hammond (2025) claims that you cannot teach the whole class reading – it should be done in small groups. That is an interesting thought, and you will find that unless your entire class is only Newcomers, you will have to teach in small groups.

> Reading and writing instruction through mini lessons is best done *with* students not *at* students.

Students are at all different stages of literacy learning; therefore, research has found that small-group instruction serves students best (Smith et al., 2022). Newcomers can be in their own small group to receive Level 1 mini lessons that will probably be on more basic literacy skills than for other students. However, some higher-proficiency ELs and native speakers who struggle with basic literacy can be grouped with Newcomers. All students benefit from mini lessons on short or long vowels, syllables, and special consonants like "y" and later get into morphology for meaning as soon as possible. Plan your mini lessons on a proactive sequence at first in the school year and later base your literacy mini lessons on the mistakes Newcomers make in writing.

Single-Point Rubrics to Grade Newcomers

Now that you have a work product from your Newcomers, you must assess as much as you can, but obviously, the amount of independent or

Table 9.3 Single-Point Rubric

More Practice	My Writing Skills	Good!
	Wrote tricky sound-letters like "y" and soft "g"	
	Wrote familiar words from class or school	
	Wrote 1–3 English sentences in subject-verb -object pattern	

semi-independent writing is far less than their peers. What grading scale and what criteria will you use? I recommend the single-point rubric for Newcomers as a template for your assessment tool and grading scale. A single-point rubric is beneficial because it is easy to develop, communicates expectations more clearly to Newcomers, and enables personalized feedback that fosters their skill development. Table 9.3 gives you one way to set up your single-point rubric.

Assignment and Topic:

Start with a three-criteria or category single-point rubric for writing tasks. Change the categories as Newcomers improve their writing. Share this with them to show growth but keep it simple and straightforward.

Multiple Criteria Single-Point Rubrics to Grade Newcomers

Add multiple criteria based on the assignment task and allow space to write feedback to your Newcomers in simple words. You should review these criteria points (grows and glows) in a conversation with your students when possible.

You can assign a point value to each category and total those points. Then, get the percentage of points earned against the total points possible for a number-to-letter grade conversion. If a Newcomer earns an 80% based on the combined scores against the total possible, that is a "B" grade. That is good work, and the Newcomer will feel more confident to try writing more academic English compared to the class rubric, which will most likely give them lower points and a lower grade. Table 9.4 shows you an example of a three-category single-point rubric with an added grading component if you wish.

Table 9.4 Single-Point Rubric with Grading Components

Working Toward Proficiency {Feedback: Areas That Need Work}	Proficient Criteria {Goals Met}	Beyond Expectations {Feedback: Evidence of Meeting or Exceeding Goals}
	Criterion One Descriptor – the specific list of performance indicators for proficiency in this area *Score: ____/total	
	Criterion Two Descriptor – the specific list of performance indicators for proficiency in this area *Score: ____/total	
	Criterion Three Descriptor – the specific list of performance indicators for proficiency in this area *Score: ____/total	

Each single-point rubric should be specific to the writing task, such as the example shown in Table 9.5, which is designed for an opinion or persuasive writing task. Note that I added categories for capitalization and punctuation because this was used later in the school year when those conventions were taught several times. This is a way to increase rigor as Newcomers gain more English proficiency.

Ready! Set! Integrate the EL Writing Process!

It is time to get started and begin your planning steps for the integration of the writing process workshop and EL Writing Process techniques. As you plan for both Newcomers and non-Newcomers, you are technically parallel planning. The differences emerge during the individual student writing steps, which may require a bit more thought and planning. While you are working with a Newcomer doing TU and PF activities, what are the

Table 9.5 Example of a Persuasive Single-Point Rubric

Need More Practice	My Writing Skills	Yes, I Wrote That!
	I can write a topic sentence that introduces . . .	
	I can write 2 reasons why I think . . .	
	I can use persuasive words in my writing.	
	I can write a topic sentence that states my topic, main points, and reasons.	
	I can write capital letters properly.	
	I can add the right punctuation in my sentences.	

other students doing? Do you have ways to keep their minds and hands busy other than a self-editing checklist which does not take much time?

Busy Hands and Minds Activities List

1. **Write a Different Ending** – Challenge them to rewrite the ending in a different way (happy, sad, surprise, twist).
2. **Post-Writing Art** – Provide extra paper for more drawing of ideas or making a comic strip from a story or expository piece.
3. **Word Work Activities** – Let them practice spelling, grammar, or vocabulary through interactive activities.
4. **Paper Art** – Make foldables or even origami shapes with instructions.
5. **Create Synonym Strings** – Have them list words or phrases from their piece and find synonyms to expand their vocabulary; put the words on index cards and hand on string like a clothesline or draw a clothesline to add the word-synonym pairs.
6. **Color-Code Your Writing** – Have students highlight different elements in their writing (e.g., verbs in green, adjectives in blue, and transition words in yellow).
7. **Quiet Games** – Have cards and other basic board games for a pair or more of students to do while others still work on writing.

My Writing Workshop Parallel Planner Class: _____ Dates:_____

Topic:_____ **Writing Task Objectives:** Write content / language objectives for the writing project.

Writing Step	Writing Process	EL Writing Process	Student Group
Prewrite	Plan and present your Seeing, Moving, Organizing Activities and Materials for Building or Retrieve Background Knowledge, Idea gathering, Brainstorming Final Model of Writing Task for non-Newcomers	Plan and present your Seeing, Moving, Organizing Activities and Level 1 English Materials for Building Background Knowledge, Idea Gathering, Vocabulary Comprehension, Group Brainstorming, in English Final Model of Writing Task for Newcomers	Whole or Small Group Instruction
Write	Write first draft with or without drawing step; answer prompt question (s) based on prewriting step activities and resources.	Draw-to-Draft activity based on Level 1 prompts and resources in prewriting step. Reminder to use WORD LINE tool, space out writing to allow for Teacher Underwriting Allow for translanguaging in first language.	Individual Activity
Edit/Revise	Peer-editing and/or peer-revising, adding drawing if time allows; write final draft with corrections and suggestions. Teacher underwriting can also be done for spelling and wording errors. Phonics Flexing can be performed as needed with non-Newcomers.	Teacher UnderWriting of first draft serving as personalized error correction focused on letter, word, phrase level English patterns. Phonics Flexing of misspelled words to serve as personalized foundational literacy instruction by flexing through each phoneme of the words you highlight	Individual Activity
Publish	Literacy mini lessons as needed by the whole class or small groups. Final draft completed to Publish works for class and/or families. Author's chair, class libraries, peer readings, and other activities that give purpose to the writing activity based on the task.	Write-to-Spell mini lessons of foundational literacy skills not yet acquired by Newcomers based on their spelling mistakes in writing. Rewrite for Repetition to interact with English patterns on paper. Publish works for class and/or families.	Whole or Small Group Instruction
Assessment	District or generic rubric of writing skills aligned to your ELA curriculum based on grade-level standards within 3-5 main categories of student writing.	Single-Point Rubric to show progress in foundational literacy of English points such as letter-sound correlation, high-frequency word spelling, or subject-verb-object basic sentence patterns. Basic grade level standards can be included. Newcomers are too new to the language for in-depth standards writing.	Teacher Activity
Notes for Next Time	Add notes for helping struggling non-Newcomer students with writing tasks.	List ideas that will help instruction flow and learning happen as you observe your Newcomers in the practice of academic English writing.	Teacher Activity

@2025, Eugenia Krimmel. Permission to copy for classroom use only.

Figure 9.1 Your writing workshop parallel planner

Plan to use one or more of these activity ideas to keep students' hands and minds busy and add them to your parallel writing planner. One thing that always bothered me when I talked about teaching ELs writing is teachers telling me they think ELs need completely different strategies and that they do not have time to plan for "those students". Once again, I cringe! There are a few differences that require purposeful planning and possibly modified materials, but overall, brains are brains, and the bilingual brain learns the same way monolingual brains do. They simply do not have the same information in their heads at the beginning, so that calls for

My Writing Workshop Parallel Planner Class: HS Science 1 Dates: 1/15 – 1/29

Topic: The Science Behind Earthquakes **Writing Task Objectives:** Describe how earthquakes occur and their effects on the environment. Use cause-and-effect structure to explain a scientific concept.

Writing Step	Writing Process	EL Writing Process	Student Group
Prewrite	Background: Review what an earthquake is Seeing: Show a video clip showing under the earth – pull key vocabulary Moving: Index cards of causes (w/ or w/o images) to match effects- put on board as word wall Organizing: Complete cause-effect organizer with information from video, images, and written sources	Background: Review what an earthquake is Seeing: Show a video clip showing under the earth – pull vocabulary from video to review Moving: Index cards with images of causes to match effects- put on board as word wall Organizing: Complete a basic Level 1 cause-effect organizer with information from video, images, and word wall words	Whole or Small Group Instruction
Write	Write a 3-paragraph first draft based on information read, watched , and added to organizer: use of WORD Line placeholder as needed: if time draw or find images that relate to the writing	Using the completed words organizer, provide 3-reason draw-to-draft organizer showing 3 causes and effects that result in an earthquake. Label each drawing with 1-2 words from word wall or bilingual dictionary. Write one sentence (3+) words for each drawing using WORD Line as needed. If time, rewrite sentences onto rough draft lined paper skipping each line – must remember.	Individual Activity
Edit/Revise	Continue to write 3 paragraphs that explore 3 causes and their effects that result in an earthquake. Fill in Word Lines. Peer review writing for editing and revision.	Teacher-Newcomer 1:1 meeting or in small groups focusing on 1 Newcomers writing at a time. Ask Newcomer to read back his/her writing; when finished review spelling through Phonics Flexing; then address grammar issues – no more than 3 at a time	Individual Activity
Publish	Rewrite corrected draft to final draft in class and add images if time allows. Pair reading of their final informative writing so listeners can identify the 3 causes and 3 effects to write on a response to listening card. Post cards on the wall. Gallery walk to look for any differences in cause-effect details. Published pieces will be posted on the hallway wall for other students to read.	Rewrite corrected draft with Phonics Flexing and grammar corrections onto the final draft paper. Tape to Newcomers drawn image if need be. Participate with all students in the gallery walk to look for any differences in cause-effect details. Published pieces will be posted on the hallway wall for other students to read.	Whole or Small Group Instruction
Assessment	Using my grade-level writing rubric with 5 categories, grade the writing according to the criteria of cause-effect structure, use of lesson's scientific words, proper punctuation and capitalization, transitions from between paragraphs, content was accurate. Grade is total points on rubric averaged for a letter grade.	Use a single-point rubric with 3 categories: Content – presented details Conventions – wrote at least 3 sentences in subj-verb-obj patter Choice of words – used lesson specific words properly Grade is total points on rubric averaged for a letter grade.	Teacher Activity
Notes for Next Time	Will complete after the workshop	Will complete after the workshop	Teacher Activity

@2025, Eugenia Krimmel. Permission to copy for classroom use only.

Figure 9.2 Completed EL writing parallel planner example

differentiation by language level, not ability level. To that end, we will practice parallel planning. Figure 9.1 illustrates a logical way to approach planning the same lesson, same unit, and same learning targets for Newcomers and non-Newcomers. I filled in a teacher's thoughts to help you with your thought process.

You will find a blank template of this parallel planner in Appendix I, and in the digital Support Materials for your everyday use. To see what your planner might look like completed, Figure 9.2 shows you an example of a parallel planner for teaching science writing to Newcomer High School students. This should only take you a few extra minutes to plan for EL writing and a few more minutes to gather or create Level 1 material for your Newcomers. Ask colleagues if they have any materials. Why not divide and conquer the work to modify for beginner Newcomers and all ELs in your school?

Next Steps for Teaching Newcomers Literacy Skills

Newcomers are known to absorb a lot of new basic English words and patterns in a short time if instruction is accessible to them. What is the next step in a Newcomer's language journey that you, as their teacher, can facilitate? They have learned words and some phrases that may be somewhat memorized, which is typical at first. However, one cannot learn an entire language by rote memory. Using the rules of English grammar and syntax, Newcomers can move behind the word stage and step into the simple to compound sentences stage of acquisition in both speaking and writing.

One tried-and-true technique for helping Newcomers move up the continuum of English literacy is what many call "expanders" as shown on Colorin Colorado (Unknown Author, (n.d.)), I have been using this technique for years, not knowing it had an actual name. I just thought it was logical to add words to the basic words Newcomers used in their writing. By adding adjectives to nouns and adverbs to verbs, we expand Newcomers' English acquisition. At the same time, you also teach parts of speech and word functions. It is a true win-win strategy.

During your mini lessons in small groups or your class of all ELs, you will present 3–5 adjectives for a lesson-related word. Add images if you can. For example, if an earthquake lesson included the word "rocks", add the adjectives "big and little". Have Newcomers write these adjective-noun pairs in their notebooks or on a handout. Then expand to a verb like "fell" with adverbs such as quickly or slowly.

Expanders start out as the most basic sentence in English, a noun and a verb.

Rocks fell.
Big rocks fell.
Big rocks fell quickly.

This is when the expanders strategy pays off by adding question words – from here, you must incorporate question words into your mini lessons because expanders add additional information for the reader! Most expanders answer the questions:

When? Where? How? How long? How much?, and Why?

Expander Pyramid Example

Boys jump.
Tall boys jump.
Tall boys jump high.
Tall boys jump high over the wall.
Tall boys jump high over the wall after school.
Tall boys jump high over the wall after school to escape from the big dogs in the neighborhood.

The last sentences give a reader the most vivid mental image and the most information. This is what you want your Newcomers to be able to do beyond the simple word stage. This will take time to build. Images help with this skill development when possible. I developed a series of shapes to indicate which type of word they can use in what order in English. Remember, grammar is not universal. Spanish, for example, has noun + adjective order while English is adjective + noun. This nonverbal way of showing Newcomers English grammar requires them to fill in the shapes to make sentences. Remember to model each step of this process. Figure 9.3 is a list of shapes and parts of speech you can reproduce for your Newcomers.

Present this "code" to the Newcomers and all your students because they may benefit from this expander activity, too. Now, build your shape expanders, as shown in Figure 9.4, to help Newcomers build sentences.

I think you get the idea of how expanders build capacity in your Newcomers to grow their English sentences for more vivid expressions of what

Noun _____	Verb ◇	Adjective ◯	Adverb △
Preposition ♡	Article (a/an/the) ⌒	Time ▭⟩	Reason Why ▭

Figure 9.3 Shapes for parts of speech expanders

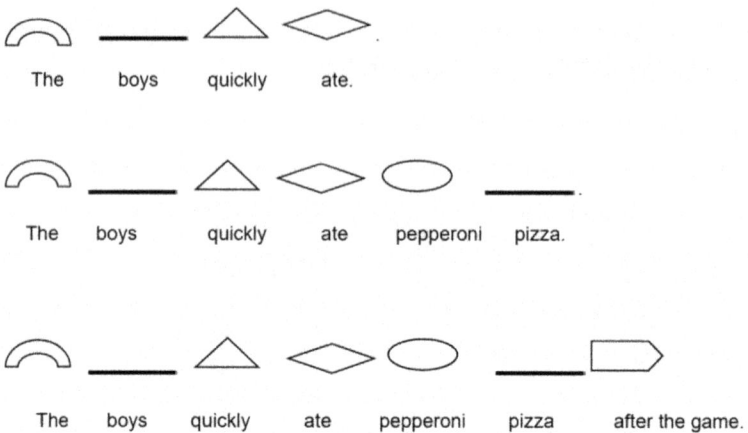

⌒ ── △ ◇ .

The   boys   quickly   ate.

⌒ ── △ ◇ ◯ ── .

The   boys   quickly   ate   pepperoni   pizza.

⌒ ── △ ◇ ◯ ── ▭⟩

The   boys   quickly   ate   pepperoni   pizza   after the game.

Figure 9.4 Examples of shape expanders for sentence building

they want to say. This is not a new technique, so you should be able to find sentence expanders practice pages and teaching materials, but truly you can make your own easily. This is a great strategy to move Newcomers beyond words.

Overall, when the EL Writing Process is integrated into your writing workshop, it accelerates Newcomers' English literacy skill development by providing the instruction they need to learn English sounds, letters, and word and phrase patterns as the foundation to their new language learning process. Teachers of Newcomers like you benefit from having a systematic approach with action steps in a logical sequence to teach phonics, spelling, and basic writing without becoming overwhelmed with time-consuming extra plans and materials. My intention of writing this book is to help you help your Newcomers – it all starts with you.

Do you think you are ready and more confident after reading this book? Take the post-assessment: Your Confidence Level Teaching Literacy to Newcomers in Appendix K. See how well you grasped the eight EL techniques within the EL Writing Process.

References

Author Unknown. (n.d.). Sentence expansion. *Colorin Colorado*. Retrieved March 6, 2025, from https://www.colorincolorado.org/teaching-ells/ell-classroom-strategy-library/sentence-expansion

Hammond, Z. (2025, March 3). *When the science of learning meets the science of reading: A multilingual approach to structured literacy* [Webinar]. edWeb.net. https://home.edweb.net/webinar/lang-lit20241022/

Orton-Gillingham.com. (n.d.). *What is the the orton-gillingham approach?* Retrieved March 9, 2025, from https://www.orton-gillingham.com/approach/#:~:text=Orton%2DGillingham%20is%20a%20step,skill%20learned%20throughout%20the%20process

Smith, K. C., Amendum, S. J., & Williams, T. W. (2022). Maximizing small-group reading instruction. *The Reading Teacher, 0*(0), 1–9.

Appendices

Appendix A
Cross-Linguistic Contrast Chart

Language	English Phoneme Difference	English Grapheme Difference	Sentence Level Differences
Arabic	- /p/ does not exist; /b/ often used for /p/ when speaking English - /v/ does not exist; /f/ often used for /v/ when speaking English - No /th/, instead says /t/ or /d/ - Consonant clusters not used; often a vowel is inserted between consonants	- "p" and "b" are often confused or interchanged until Arabic speaker is unsure of how to write the /p/ sound. - No upper/lower case; only consonants & long vowels are written; short vowels are diacritical marks - Right-left directionality - 3 forms of written letters depending on position in word: initial, middle, and end	- No use of "to be". i.e. I am a student (ENG); "I student" in Arabic - Sentence patterns are flexible with subjects or objects first. - Adjective after noun: "house white", not "white house" - No modals (can, could, would, etc.)
Chinese Mandarin	- No /v/, /z/, and /r/ sounds - have no difference in vowel length; no long and short vowels - Struggle to hear or say difference of "beat" and "bit", "bean" and "bin"	- Non-alphabetic writing system: however, pinyin alphabet was adopted in 1950s for signs, children's books, etc. Pinyin consists of Latin script letters: a b c ch d e f g h i j k l m n o p q r s sh t u w x y z zh (now used with digital writing like texting)	- Verbs do not hold "time" or tense; time expressions or adverbial phrases indicate time/tense - No use of "to be" with adjectives (*The man intelligent.*)

(Continued)

(Continued)

Language	English Phoneme Difference	English Grapheme Difference	Sentence Level Differences
	- No short /a/ sound; uses short /u/ or short /e/ instead - No short /u/; confuses "Luke" and "look" - /b/, /d/, and /p/ are voiceless and barely pronounced at all - No /v/ exists; instead use /w/ or /f/ - /n/ does not exist in all dialects; difficult to hear/ say "night" from "light" - No /th/, instead says /t/d/s/ - /z/ does not exist in most dialects; will use /s/ instead - /l/ and /r/ are not distinguished; hard to hear/say - Final consonants rare in words; will drop final consonant to say only vowel or will add vowel sound to English word - Few clusters or sound combinations exist; will add vowels for harmony	- Over 8,000 characters in simplified Chinese alphabet - English spelling patterns/rules are difficult to acquire - Words made up of one or more syllables; each syllable is represented by a single character - Individual words take longer time to decipher than ideograms - Flexible writing directionality; usually right-left vertically. Also found left-right horizontally; newspapers use all directions - No articles "a/an, the" exist - No gender exists; often mix up pronouns - Plurals are not suffixes; -s often dropped when writing plurals in English (no concept); plurals indicated by repeat of noun or number before noun	- No use of auxiliary verbs in negatives or questions - Modals do not have the same meaning when used for polite registry in English (Would you mind . . .?), so they sound abrupt (EN: *Would you like to eat?* CH: *You would like to eat?*) - Format of questions do not change or invert like English; the question is a sentence said in the tone and context; with the addition of a question word in some cases

(Continued)

(Continued)

Language	English Phoneme Difference	English Grapheme Difference	Sentence Level Differences
French	- Most consonants at the end of words are not pronounced including plural /s/ sounds - /r/ is softer and almost silent in French - /th/ does not exist; will use /t/d/s/z/ instead - /h/ is silent - No short /i/ sound; instead, long /e/ is used - /ch/ phoneme less common; often pronounced like /sh/	- No "k" or "w" written in French words - Last consonant letter of French words not spoken; therefore, ending sounds are dropped in English - French includes accented vowels that in English are the same symbol but have differing word stress - Long /e/ written with "i" - Several vowels have various written forms like English vowels, but not the same letters (i.e. /a/ has 8 spellings in English; 6 in French)	- Nouns are masculine or feminine - Comparative and superlative adjectives only use word indicators: more or most (no suffix) - No auxiliary verb "do" - Verb negative uses 2 words "ne ___ pas" - Two or more adjectives have "and" in between *i.e., a short and red dress* - No present or future progressive verb tense - Typical use infinitive verb with modal *i.e., can swim = can to swim* - Noun before adjective *i.e., house white EN: white house* - Possessive uses *of*-phrases not *'s i.e., "John's book" is "a/the book of John"* [le livre de John]

(Continued)

(Continued)

Language	English Phoneme Difference	English Grapheme Difference	Sentence Level Differences
German	- German speakers confuse the sounds /e/ and /æ/ which can cause words like "pet" and "pat" - /w/ is often pronounced as /v/ - /j/ and /ch/ are rare in German - /z/, /v/, /g/, /b/, and /d/ not common at end of German words, so will substitute other sounds - /th/ does not exist; will use /t/d/s/z/ instead	- These letters represent English short vowels in German: ä, ö, and ü. - /w/ and /v/ are often interchanged because German has neither /w/ nor "w" - "v" and "f" are also interchanged in writing - Plural endings are -en and -er, not -s - More compound words than in English that are written in two words	- No auxiliary verb "do" - Negative verb form is *verb + nicht (not)* - No present or future progressive verb tense, *going to* future - No -ing form of words - Verbs usually come to end of clause or sentence - Direct object can start a sentence, not a subject - Article may be separated from noun by phrases not just adjectives like in English *i.e., "the family budget" – GR: "the of the family budget"* - Indefinite articles (a/an) often omitted
Spanish	- /v/ and /b/ are pronounced the same - /j/ is written "y" in Spanish and "j" is pronounced /hota/. - /h/ is silent - /z/ pronounced /th/ in Spain and /s/ in Latin Spanish	- "v" and "b" are interchanged often - "i" is written for any long /e/ sound including the "y" as /ee/. - /j/ sound is not written "y"	- noun before adjective i.e. house white unlike English white house - Use of gender/ plural definite articles "el, la, los, las" before nouns

(*Continued*)

(Continued)

Language	English Phoneme Difference	English Grapheme Difference	Sentence Level Differences
	- /k/ for "qu", not /kw/ - /th/ exists in dialect of central Spain, but not in other dialects; speakers will use /t/d/s/z/ instead	- Initial /s/ cluster sounds take on the "e" to make the Spanish pronunciation rule /es/, /est/, /esp/ - "H" not often written by Spanish speakers	- Preposition "en" translates to *in, on, at* - No contractions in Spanish - Possessives use *of*-phrases not *'s i.e., "John's book" is "a/the book of John" [el libro de John]*
Turkish	- Phoneme pattern is consonant-vowel-consonant without double letters or clusters; borrowed words may have clusters - /v/ is used for English /w/ and /v/ because no /w/ - /ou/ as in "low" is pronounced closer to "law" - Vowels are "a, e, ı, i, o, ö, u, ü"; no short /a/, long /i/ - /r/ changes sound depending on position; at end of word /r/ is softened and devoiced - /th/ does not exist; will use /t/d/ instead - /b/, /d/, and /dg/ lose voice in final position	- /j/ is written with "c" - No "x" exists; "ks" is used for borrowed words like "taxi = taksi" - no "q" or "w" - /ch/ is written with a Ç in Turkish and /sh/ symbol is Ş - Written vowels are "a, e, ı, i, o, ö, u, ü" – long /a/= "ay", long /i/="ay", "ö and ü" are elongated = long /o/, /u/ phonemes, short /o/, /u/ = "o and u" - Clusters, diphthongs, and diagraphs pose problems in writing because of vowel/sound harmony rules	- Sentence pattern is subject-object-verb - Subject sometimes only indicated through conjugation of verb in conversation, i.e. "I went home". Turkish = Ev'e gittim (Home to went (I) verb conjugated to indicate 1st person singular - Plural end "-lar or -ler" are used based on vowel harmony with the proceeding syllable type – back or front vowel

(*Continued*)

(Continued)

Language	English Phoneme Difference	English Grapheme Difference	Sentence Level Differences
	- /g/ does not occur at end of words; /k/ sound is added to borrowed words - System of back vowels and front vowels constitute vowel harmony - Word stress on last syllable usually unlike English	- No form of "the" used, "a/an" sometimes placed between adjective and noun - Comparatives and superlatives use separate words, no suffix	- Prepositions follow the noun and are often attached as a suffix - Verbs show person, number, tense, and modality - No gender in pronouns or verb forms - "to be" verb rarely used; "there is/are" is used instead - Specific suffix for expressing the state of being of each pronoun case - No "to have" verb; use "there is/are" instead - Auxiliary verbs in English are confusing and often omitted
Another Language	- You fill	Add information about the languages of your Newcomers not already noted in this book. Start with https://omniglot.com/ or https://www.ethnologue.com/	
Another Language		-	-

Appendix B
EL Writing Survey – Tracking Record

Student   Name: _____Grade_____ 1st

Language_____

Date Tested	1	2	% ↑↓	3	% ↑↓	4	% ↑↓	Notes
Phonological Awareness								
A. Letter-Sound Recognition (-/6)								
B. Blending Sounds (-/6)								
C. Onset-Rimes Omission (-/6)								
Phonics								
D. Letter Recognition Uppercase (-/26)								
E. Letter Recognition Lowercase (-/26)								
F. Digraph Recognition (-/6)								
G. Word Families (-/10)								
H. Jobs of "Y" (-/6)								
Decoding								
I. Short Vowels/CVC (-/5)								
J. Long Vowels/VCe (-/5)								
K. R-controlled words (-/5)								
L. Read Blends (-/9)								
M. Read Digraphs (-/6)								
N. Multisyllabic Words (-/6)								
Encoding								
O. EL Spelling Inventory (-/8)								
Observations:								

Appendix C
Teacher Instructions for NLS

Phonological Awareness	This segment is to assess knowledge of basic English sounds. There are no written words for this section.
A. Letter-Sound Recognition (-/6)	Tell student: I will say a word and repeat the first sound. Repeat the first sound of the letter after me. Example: I say "pet" first sound is "p". Please repeat that sound. 1. may /m/ sound 4. let / l/ sound 2. pin /p/ sound 5. bed /b/ sound 3. dim /d/ sound 6. wish /w/ sound
B. Blending Sounds (-/6)	We will say 2 or 3 sounds blended to make a word like in /h/ + /ē/ = "he". Your turn: please say these sounds together: 1. /n/ + /ō/ = ? 4. /k/+/ō/+/d/ = ? 2. /m/ + /ī/ = ? 5. /s/+/ă/+/g/ =? 3. /ĭ/ + /t/ = ? 6. /sp/+/ĕ/+/ll/ =?
C. Onset-Rimes Omission (-/6)	I will say a word, then say it again without the first sound: example – "bike"/-ike without the /b/. Your turn, say these words without the first sound: 1. "car" = /are/ 4. "peas" = /ease/ 2. "take" = /ake/ 5. "fog" = /og/ 3. "row" = /ō/ 6. "sip" = /ĭp/
Phonics	This segment is to assess letter and word recognition from speech. It is not reading from the written word.
D. Letter Recognition Uppercase (-/26)	Circle the letters a student recognizes when you point to these letters in the Student Booklet which has them in a random order. A B C D E F G H I J K L M N O P Q R S T U V W X Y Z

E. Letter Recognition Lowercase (-/26)	Circle the letters a student recognizes when you point to these letters in the Student Booklet which has them in a random order. a b c d e f g h i j k l m n o p q r s t u v w x y z
F. Digraph Recognition (-/6)	Minimal pairs activity: Show students to circle only one of the words when they hear you say a word. Example: Student Booklet has 2 words in a row: shoe and chew – you say "shoe"; student must circle only "shoe" on the page. 1. "Chip" 4. "Dose" 2. "Share" 5. "Wheel" 3. "This" 6. "Vale pronounced "veil""
G. Word Families (-/10)	Pronounce the words here on your teacher page. Students see 3 words in the Booklet. Ask them to tell you which word rhymed with the word you said. Example: "sat" (in Teacher page only). Read the 3 words while pointing to each. Ask student to tell you which rhymes with "sat" – mad, pat, bet by saying/repeating the word. If student points to a word, ask them to read the word aloud. 1. "**man**" – mat, let, pan 4. "**not**" – met, pit, got 2. "**thin**" – bin, that, his 5. "**cut**" – nut, cub, cod 3. "**bed**" – ben, red, ran
Decoding	This segment of the assessment is to determine if they can read aloud or decode letters of letter combinations in English.
H. Short Vowels/CVC (-/5)	Tell students to read the words in row H of the Student Booklet. Record the number of correctly pronounced words listening for the short vowel sound. Do not pronounce these for the student.
I. Long Vowels/VCe (-/5)	Tell students to read the words in row I of the Student Booklet. Record the number of correctly pronounced words listening for the short vowel sound. Do not pronounce these for the student.
J. R-controlled words (-/5)	Tell students to read the words in row J of the Student Booklet. Record the number of correctly pronounced words listening for the short vowel sound. Do not pronounce these for the student.
K. Read Blends (-/9)	Tell students to read the words in row K of the Student Booklet. Record the number of correctly pronounced words listening for the short vowel sound. Do not pronounce these for the student.

L. Read Digraphs (-/6)	Tell students to read the words in row L of the Student Booklet. Record number of correctly pronounced words listening for the short vowel sound. Do not pronounce these for the student.
M. Multisyllabic Words (-/6)	Tell students to read the words in row M of the Student Booklet. Record number of correctly pronounced words listening for the short vowel sound. Do not pronounce these for the student.
Encoding	This segment is to observe what sound-letter correlation the student knows in English by spelling these words. You are looking for the spelling of certain sounds or patterns.
N. EL Spelling Inventry (-/8)	EL Spelling Inventory is the last page of the Student Booklet. Ask students to write each word for the picture. You can pronounce the words before the student starts writing so they can hear the phonemes. Then do not give any further help. Allow students to write as they think it should be spelled in English. Words in order are: Monkey, frog, dress, eagle, horse, apple, catfish, jumped

Basic Writing Skills Survey: Sentence/Question level Triumphs and Trials		
Skills Survey	**Triumphs Recorded**	**Trials Recorded**
Basic S-V, S-V-O* pattern		
Proper use of pronouns		
Proper capitalization		
Proper ending punctuation		
Correct word order adj + noun, question form*		
Observations:		

* English sentence patterns: S-V-O = Subject-Verb-Object sentence structure common in English sentence patterns or * Question structures: Open-ended with "W" words or closed with Auxiliary Verb + Subject + Verb + Object? (AV-S-V-O).

Appendix D
Student Booklet – Newcomer Literacy Survey

Student Name:	Grade:	Date of Test:

Boxes A, B, and C have no written English.

Phonics

D	U Z G K Y D I Q C N S M F V B J H O A R E X T L P W
E	k h s w c b e q g a y r u l t p n o d v x j i f z m
F	Circle 1 word you hear for each line. Example: Shoe Chew 1. Ship Chip 2. Chair Share 3. This Dish 4. Dose Those 5. Wheel Veal 6. Vale Whale
G	Circle 1 word that rhymes for each line. Example: mad, pat, bet 1. mat let pan 2. bin that his 3. ben red ran 4. met pit got 5. nut cub cod

Decoding	
H	nap men six got cod
I	tale note line mem dune
J	star her fir purr for
K	sled glad trip drink snap stop
L	chant back king shop thing what
M	carpet napkin pencil water zero

N. Encoding – EL Spelling Inventory   Write the word of each photo.

Notes:

Appendix E
Explanatory/Opinion Graphic Organizer

Name: _____   Date: _____

I like to

Favorite Activities Word Splash

Reason/Detail 1	Reason/Detail 2	Reason/Detail 3
_____	_____	_____
_____	_____	_____
_____	_____	_____
_____	_____	_____
_____	_____	_____

This Level 1 graphic organizer can be used for opinion, descriptive, or informative writing. Newcomers can record words from the pre-writing stage when you introduce key words, or they can translate as they wish. The "I like" sentence starter box is to narrow the topic of writing. That starter can change to the writing task topic.

The personalized word splash section allows Newcomers time to gather English words and phrases from the pre-writing activities. The three boxes for opinion can be titled "reason" or "detail" for informative writing.

Newcomers have now organized their thoughts onto paper. On another page, they can write out their English sentences to give their opinion, describe something, or even provide information.

Appendix F
Narrative Graphic Organizer for Level 1

My Name: _____   My Story Title:_____

Draw-to-Draft

Beginning	Middle	End
Who? *My brother*	Who?	Who?
Do? *run*	Do?	Do?
What? *train for visit grandmom*	What?	What?

My Story Title:

_____ by

_____ (your name: author)

_____

_____

_____

This graphic organizer uses the *Who? Do? What? Strategy*. Newcomers draw what they are thinking to create a three-part story. You or a partner ask them to answer the three questions about each image they drew.

Newcomers write words to answer **who do**es or is **do**ing **what** in the picture that they drew. This makes the activity accessible to a Level 1 EL. From there show them how to string these words together to make a properly ordered English sentence.

Appendix G
Skipped Lines
Four-Part Graphic
Organizer

	X (do not write in this line)
	X
	X
	X (do not write in this line)
	X
	X
	X (do not write in this line)
	X
	X
	X (do not write in this line)
	X
	X

This Level 1 graphic organizer can be used for writing about either a topic with a three-step process or a topic with two details and a conclusion. The possibilities are numerous. The value of this organizer is Newcomers can draw and write on the same page. The X lines allow space for better teacher underwriting and phonics flexing. It also serves as a model for skipping lines if you hand out notebook paper. All these things must be demonstrated because Newcomers do not understand at this early stage of exposure to English.

Appendix H
Single-Point Rubric Template

Single-Point Rubric   **Assignment and Topic:**

More Practice	My Writing Skills	Good!
	Wrote tricky sound-letters like "y" and soft "g"	
	Wrote familiar words from class or school	
	Wrote 1–3 English sentences in subject-verb-object pattern	

Single-point rubric with three criteria or categories of writing to focus on in that writing workshop. Change the categories as Newcomers improve their writing. Share this with them to show growth, but keep it simple and straightforward.

Add a Score per Category

More Practice	My Writing Skills	Good!
	Wrote tricky sound-letters like "y" and soft "g" Score: _____/3	
	Wrote familiar words from class or school Score: _____/3	
	Wrote 1–3 English sentences in subject-verb-object pattern Score: _____/3	

Appendix I
My Writing Workshop Parallel Planner

Class: _____ Dates:_____

Topic:_____ Writing Task Objectives:

Writing Step	Writing Process	EL Writing Process	Student Group
Prewrite			Whole or Small-Group Instruction
Write			Individual Activity
Edit/Revise			Individual Activity
Publish			Whole or Small-Group Instruction
Assessment			Teacher Activity
Notes for Next Time			Teacher Activity

Source: @2025, Eugenia Krimmel. Permission to copy for classroom use only.

Appendix J
Sentence Expander Words and Phrases Examples

Add information to your sentence by question		
When?	• in the afternoon/morning/evening • at night • next year/week/month	• every day/week/year • this morning/afternoon • yesterday/tomorrow • later
Where?	• at school • in the country • in my mind • in space	• in the forest • in my backyard • over there • in the United States
Why?	• because I can . . . • to finish my homework • to escape . . .	• to get help • to call home • because they need my . . .
How?	• quickly • fast • loudly	• slowly • clearly • energetically
How much?	• more/most • a lot of • a majority of	• a little • a few • none
How long?	• so far • since last night • until tomorrow	• for a year/week/month • 5 times • always/never

Appendix K
Teaching Confidence Post-Assessment

Post-Assessment

This survey is also found in editable form in the Support Materials folder for this book.

Instructions: Please read each statement and rate your confidence level on a scale of

1 = low, 2 = medium, and 3 = high confidence.

1. I feel confident in my ability to teach basic phonics concepts to Newcomer students.
   1 – Low
   2 – Medium
   3 – High
2. I am knowledgeable about effective strategies for teaching spelling to Newcomer students, considering their language proficiency level.
   1 – Low
   2 – Medium
   3 – High
3. I feel confident in my ability to scaffold writing instruction for Newcomer students, helping them develop basic writing skills.
   1 – Low
   2 – Medium
   3 – High

4. I understand how to differentiate instruction in phonics, spelling, and writing to meet the diverse needs of Newcomer students.
   1 – Low
   2 – Medium
   3 – High
5. I am comfortable assessing Newcomer students' progress in phonics, spelling, and writing and using assessment data to inform my instruction.
   1 – Low
   2 – Medium
   3 – High
6. I feel confident in my ability to create engaging and culturally responsive learning activities for teaching phonics, spelling, and writing to Newcomer students.
   1 – Low
   2 – Medium
   3 – High
7. I actively seek out professional development opportunities to enhance my understanding of teaching phonics, spelling, and writing to Newcomer students.
   1 – Low
   2 – Medium
   3 – High
8. I understand the importance of providing explicit instruction and ample practice opportunities in phonics, spelling, and writing for Newcomer students to build their skills effectively.
   1 – Low
   2 – Medium
   3 – High
9. I feel confident in my ability to support Newcomer students who may have limited prior literacy experiences in their native language.
   1 – Low
   2 – Medium
   3 – High

10. Overall, I feel confident in my ability to teach basic academic phonics, spelling, and writing skills to Newcomer students.

    1 – Low

    2 – Medium

    3 – High

Total: Number of each score _____x 1s + _____x 2s + _____x 3s =

Total Score _____/30 possible points

Your Confidence Rating:

1–10: Still in Need of More Understanding and Building My Confidence in Literacy Teaching!

- I read this book from cover to cover to gain a comprehensive understanding of language acquisition concepts and EL-centered literacy techniques but still need to visualize it in action. I would benefit from watching a colleague using these techniques to reinforce my understanding and receive direct feedback on my teaching practice based on what I read in this book.

I would benefit from in-person training to reinforce my understanding and receive direct feedback on my teaching practice based on what I read in this book.

11–20: Somewhat Confident in How to Teach Literacy to Newcomers but Still Learning!

- I read this book cover to cover to grasp the fundamental concepts and strategies thoroughly. I understood the principles and reasons for each step of the EL Writing Process but am only somewhat confident that I can incorporate these techniques effectively. I will incorporate one at a time to get better at teaching my Newcomers basic English literacy skills.

- I would feel more confident with how-to in-person, synchronous, or asynchronous training courses but may also seek additional resources or support from experienced EL writing teachers as needed.

21–30: Teaching Literacy Instruction to Newcomers No Longer Baffles Me!

- I will jump right into integrating the EL Writing Process protocol into my next writing workshop routine. I will use the EL Writing Parallel Planner to help me set up strategies and gather appropriate Level 1 materials to provide accessible literacy learning for my Newcomers.
- I will observe how well and how quickly my Newcomers will acquire English reading and writing skills by teaching phonics, spelling, and writing through integrated EL writing techniques compared to my Newcomers who did not receive the integrated instruction.
- I will share the results with my colleagues and school leaders to help other educators understand the value of teaching Newcomers of any age basic foundational skills as part of the grade-level instructional routine.

For Product Safety Concerns and Information please contact our EU
representative GPSR@taylorandfrancis.com
Taylor & Francis Verlag GmbH, Kaufingerstraße 24, 80331 München, Germany

www.ingramcontent.com/pod-product-compliance
Ingram Content Group UK Ltd.
Pitfield, Milton Keynes, MK11 3LW, UK
UKHW021650170925
462995UK00020B/607

9 7 8 1 0 4 1 0 0 5 8 3 4